W9-CAY-823

Struggle Seek Grow

Struggle Seek Grow

How 12 Women in Scripture
Sought Spiritual Maturity

Cynthia Dianne Guy

Gospel Advocate Company
Nashville, Tennessee

Also by Cynthia Dianne Guy

What About the Women?

© 2011 by Gospel Advocate Co.

IT IS ILLEGAL AND UNETHICAL TO DUPLICATE COPYRIGHTED MATERIAL.

All scripture quotations, unless otherwise noted, are taken from the HOLY BIBLE: NEW KING JAMES VERSION. © 1988 Thomas Nelson Inc. Used by permission. All rights reserved.

Some scriptures quoted are taken from the HOLY BIBLE: EASY-TO-READ VERSION ETRV © 2001 by World Bible Translation Center, Inc. Used by permission.

All rights reserved. No part of this publication may be reproduced, stored in a retrieval system or transmitted in any form or by any means – electronic, mechanical, photocopy, recording, or any other – except for brief quotations in printed reviews, without the prior permission of the publisher.

Published by Gospel Advocate Co.
1006 Elm Hill Pike, Nashville, TN 37210
www.gospeladvocate.com

ISBN 10: 0-89225-580-3
ISBN 13: 978-0-89225-580-1

*This study is lovingly dedicated to
four special Christian women:
my daughters-in-law,
Mindy, Kristina, Lacey and Taylor;
and my granddaughters,
Sofia and Abby-Brooke.*

Table of Contents

Introduction
to the Study

*A*re you out of shape? Have you stood in front of a mirror and thought, "I need to exercise"? Even with available fitness centers and workout videos, many of us struggle. The same may be true spiritually. Many sigh, "I'm not as close to God as I want to be" or "I wish I could overcome my spiritual problem with ... ." Paul tells us that training in godliness is even better than bodily exercise because it offers a better life now and in eternity (1 Timothy 4:7-8). Motivation and consistency in spiritual fitness are essential. But in this, too, we struggle.

Scripture teaches us how to improve one's desire and ability to grow spiritually. It provides examples of women who allowed God's Word to penetrate their hearts and transform their lives into Christlikeness. But such "spiritual formation" did not come without struggle. Each faced specific trials of life by seeking help from above. Childless Hannah deflected self-pity and Peninnah's taunts as she poured out her heart to God. Bitter Naomi blamed God for the loss of her husband and sons, but sought relief within His law and people. Helpless Hagar, desperate to save her child, lifted up her voice and wept. Each struggled. Each sought. Each grew.

Their "spiritual formation" resulted from engaging in specific maturity-building exercises such as prayer, listening to God's Word, service, etc. John Ortberg asserts, "Authentic spiritual transformation begins with training, with discipline."[1] Because the Greek word for "exercise" (*gumnasia*, from which *gymnastics* derives) may also be translated "discipline" (1 Timothy 4:7-8 NASB), the term "spiritual disciplines" is often used as "a shorthand expression for the spiritual practices that Scripture expects of God's people."[2]

This book presents 12 biblical models of the practice of spiritual disciplines. My prayer is that you will be inspired to imitate these women and to engage in these exercises. Then you, too, may become spiritually mature as life's trials motivate you to struggle, seek and grow.

Attentive Listening
Mary of **Bethany**

Luke 10:38-42

The Weaver twins had finally arrived. Our church family was ecstatic! We had prayed together through some anxious moments – when contractions came too early and when little Anniston seemed to stop growing. Kelly followed her doctor's orders for rest and nourishment with fervent prayer. Happily, both babies were born with healthy appetites. In time they put on the expected pounds, and we were thankful. Babies are supposed to grow.

This concept is true also in the spiritual realm. Every Christian begins as a babe in Christ. The Scriptures urge us to "grow in the grace and knowledge of our Lord and Savior Jesus Christ" (2 Peter 3:18). But Satan works hard to discourage zeal and commitment. He tempts us to set spiritual nourishment aside and seek satisfaction elsewhere such as in material possessions, popularity, career and relationships with other people. These, however, do not sustain us. Gordon T. Smith beautifully explains, "The words of Jesus are the bread by which we live (John 6), the living water for which we thirst (7:37-38) and the light of the world (8:12). He is water, bread and light to those who listen to his voice."[1]

Spiritual maturity comes through attentive listening to Jesus through Scripture. Have you experienced growth in regular Bible study? Or do you identify with those who were baptized years ago but remain unskilled in God's Word? If you feel stagnant and immature spiritually, you are not alone.

In 2001, John Ellis conducted a survey of Christians in Memphis, Tenn., and found that the No. 1 felt need among 614 adults was a desire for "enriching their spiritual life."[2] Ellis noted, "Members are hungering to know how to draw closer to God, and they want help."[3] It appears that many failed to receive such help. *The Christian Chronicle* reported in March 2009 that the church experienced a 4.7 percent drop – 526 fewer congregations and 78,436 fewer members – between 2003 and 2009.[4]

Interestingly, two studies from Regent University (2003) and at the University of California-Los Angeles Higher Education Research Institute (2005) showed that American women possess great spiritual hunger. Compared to men, their statistics reveal, women seem to be more concerned and more engaged in personal spiritual quests.[5] Then, why is the church losing members?

Charlton Hillis asserts that large numbers of women are spiritually undernourished. In an article titled "Women's Bible Classes: Fluff or Substance," Hillis observes,

> A common picture at our lectureships and seminars is a Greek scholar expounding upon the meaning of the text to a roomful of men and only a handful of women. The majority of women have gone off to a women's class which, if true to norm, makes no pretense at scholarliness. All too often, "uplifting but light" describes the menu for these classes.[6]

Is it true, as Hillis suggests, that Bible classes and literature often leave the impression that domestic activities are the totality of spiritual fulfillment for women? Some older women admit that "a lifetime of activities like church dinners had taken the place of spiritual growth."[7] Many younger women explain that their busy schedules hinder time for Bible study. Jesus addresses this issue in Luke 10 during His visit with Mary and Martha.

The Scriptures' Message

Perhaps you are familiar with this reminder of spiritual priorities. Martha may be applauded for her hospitality, but Mary's attentiveness to Jesus' words received commendation. Mary chose the "good part" when she took the opportunity to listen to Jesus (Luke 10:42). Nourishment that promotes spiritual maturity comes from Scripture (1 Peter 2:2).

Jesus visited Mary and Martha in Bethany. Luke wrote, "Martha welcomed Him into her house" (Luke 10:38). This suggests Martha was the homeowner and perhaps the older sister. Mary "also sat at Jesus' feet and heard His word. But Martha was distracted with much serving" (vv. 39-40). It appears that both sisters sat and talked with their guest, but Martha became sidetracked. According to birth-order literature, the oldest child tends to be conscientious, well-organized and somewhat critical.[8] Those of us in this category understand Martha's feeling of responsibility to provide for Jesus' needs. However, by focusing on the physical she was missing a spiritual feast.

The Greek imperfect verbs denote that Mary *continued* to listen to Jesus while Martha – instead of giving Him her full attention – perhaps *continued* to be distracted with the tasks of "much serving" (Luke 10:40). We can imagine Martha leaving Jesus' presence to check on the bread or cover the steaming vegetables. Maybe she went out to the garden, washed some dishes and set the table. Do you ever become distracted while studying His Word? Mary, on the other hand, *continued* listening to Jesus. R.C.H. Lenski described the scene:

> The moment Jesus indicated that he had something to impart Mary turned from everything else to sit and to be absorbed in what he said. This natural, devoted, devout, complete attention to Jesus' Word stands through all the ages of the church as the true mark of

discipleship. To receive the doctrine of Jesus with a docile heart is better than any work, labor, sacrifice, or suffering. To close the ear, to turn the heart away, no matter what the cause, is bound to be fatal, for it shuts off the life stream on which our faith depends.[9]

Mary provides a model of attentive listening to the Word. Jesus was the Word who "became flesh" (John 1:14). Mary sat at His feet. This posture was not merely physical. In Scripture the phrase "[t]o be seated (passive aorist participle) at the feet" meant "to act as a pupil."[10] Paul was brought up "at the feet of Gamaliel" and was taught according to the law of the fathers (Acts 22:3). Mary placed herself in the role of pupil and Jesus as teacher.

Although we are not in His physical presence, we have opportunities today to sit at Jesus' feet through study and meditation on Scripture. But, like Martha, we can become distracted, trying to make time for the Word while taking care of daily tasks. Life pulls us away. It takes deliberate effort to make time for study. Paul encourages us to "serve the Lord without distraction" (1 Corinthians 7:35). We often need a reminder of what is important.

Jesus gives this reminder in Luke 10. As Martha worked she became impatient with Mary's lack of assistance and asked Jesus, "Lord, do You not care that my sister has left me to serve alone? Therefore tell her to help me" (v. 40). Jesus' answer must have surprised her. He affirmed Mary's priority of listening and challenged, "Martha, Martha, you are worried and troubled about many things. But one thing is needed, and Mary has chosen that good part, which will not be taken away from her" (vv. 41-42).

First, Jesus doubled Martha's name. Deity often did this to get someone's attention. Notice the calls to Moses (Exodus 3:4), Samuel (1 Samuel 3:10), and Saul of Tarsus (Acts 9:4). Next, Jesus gently rebuked Martha's "anxiety-ridden entertaining."[11] She was much too concerned with the details of serving. Jesus described Martha as "worried" (*merimnas*), referring to her mental distraction, and "troubled" (*thorubazo*), denoting external agitation.[12] Martha was stressed out mentally and physically. A gentle reminder was necessary for Martha and continues for those of us with a "Martha streak."[13]

I am reminded of an elderly woman visited by her preacher. She got up to offer him coffee, then to serve cookies, and again to get him a napkin. He gently chided, "Martha, I don't want coffee, I don't want cookies, and I don't want a napkin. I want you to sit down and talk with me." Guests are only as comfortable as the hostess. I'm sure Jesus would have preferred a sandwich on a paper plate instead of perfect pasta under pressure.

Martha was worried and troubled while the solution to her distress was right in front of her. She could have found relief simply by sitting at the feet of Jesus. He is the source of peace. The psalmist wrote, "I will hear what God the LORD will speak, For He will speak peace To His people and to His saints" (Psalm 85:8). Lenski observed that "anxiety and a troubled mind are corrected only by having Jesus substitute the one needful thing which then works calmness and quiet assurance from above."[14]

During this precious hour, Martha's mind was divided – *part* on the spiritual and *part* on the physical. Mary, however, chose to focus on the good *part* – the "one thing" needed (Luke 10:42). Martha had the same opportunity, but she missed it. We too may choose to emulate Martha's troubled mind or Mary's attentive listening. Which one provides peace?

The Maturity-Building Discipline of Bible Study

The "good part" is spiritual nourishment found in the Word. Jesus said in Matthew 4:4, "Man shall not live by bread alone, but by every word that proceeds from the mouth of God." Calling himself the Bread of Life, He urged, "He who comes to Me shall never hunger, and He who believes on Me shall never thirst" (John 6:35). Matthew 6:33 promises that if we "seek first the kingdom of God and His righteousness," we will receive all the things we need. And regular feeding on Scripture builds faith in His ability to provide.

If we understand how important the Bible is to our lives, we will be motivated to study it. Adele Cayhoun insightfully wrote:

> The Bible is divine revelation. God's own word to us. It reveals who God is, who we are and why we are here. Through Bible study we gain insights into God, human nature and creation. Studying the Scriptures can equip, guide and reveal how to live in life-giving ways that deepen our friendship with God and others. Both Old and New Testaments encourage regular study, meditation, contemplation and memorization of God's Word. The benefits of Bible study are directly related to how open, attentive and obedient we are to what we read.[15]

The Bible explains how to have a happy, spiritually healthy life. It provides knowledge about God (John 14:9), answers to life's questions (2 Timothy 3:16-17), protection against Satan's temptations (Psalm 119:11; Ephesians 6:11), guidance in making right decisions (Jeremiah 10:23; Psalm 119:105), strength in trials of life (46:1), and a map for a blessed eternity (John 5:39). God provided the Scriptures – not just for religious leaders and Bible teachers, but for everyone to study (2 Timothy 2:15). Mary of Bethany was not an expert in spirituality. She was just hungry for the Bread of Life.

Mary's attentive listening required preparation. Anthony Fischetto, in *Transformed: Intimacy With God*, urges Christians to "Follow the Mary Factor," that is, "Mary sat at Jesus' feet. … She mentally decided to listen, physically prepared herself to sit at Jesus' feet, which then prepared her spiritually to receive God's Word."[16] It's a matter of priority. Fischetto adds,

> We can always take the time given to us by God and return a portion of it to him by spending personal time with him. Not just a token prayer, a quick reading of a Bible verse, or the busyness of church life, but a true commitment to the Almighty and a conscious decision to "Be still, and know that [He is] God" (Psalm 46:10).[17]

The following suggestions may help you prepare for Bible study. They were developed from Rosemary Whittle McKnight's ideas in her book *I Love Me, I Love Me Not*.[18]

(1) *Make an appointment for personal time in the Word.* Set your alarm 15 minutes early, or place the Bible next to your bed for nightly reading. Plan a refreshing study session during your lunch or break time. Arrive at your child's school 15 minutes early to read while you wait. Make a regular appointment to sit at Jesus' feet. He'll be there waiting for you.

(2) *Have a plan for personal time in the Word.* Choose a daily reading program or a devotional guide from a Christian publisher. Enjoy a topical study using a Bible concordance, topical Bible, pictorial Bible encyclopedia, etc. Consult your church library or Bible bookstore for good commentaries for textual study through a book of the Bible. Study for a class you are teaching or one you attend. Imagine what the quality of Bible classes would be if everyone came prepared. Take and review notes from sermons. The Bereans were commended for their personal study (Acts 17:10-11). I recommend Sue Crabtree's chapter titled "Bible Study" in *Woman to Woman*.

(3) *Make use of idle moments for personal time in the Word.* When your hands are busy and your mind is free (driving, cleaning, etc.), listen to recorded Bible readings or lectures. Place texts for memorizing above the kitchen sink, on the bathroom mirror or in your purse. Keep a small Bible handy to read while waiting for appointments.

Attentive listening to God's Word produces spiritual maturity. The writer of Hebrews urged Christians to "go on to perfection" (Hebrews 6:1). "Perfection," in the Greek here, means a complete or high level of maturity.[19] In his article, "Indications of Immaturity," Martel Pace explains:

The maturity that the writer desired for the Christians to whom he wrote was a capability to grasp and appreciate the exposition of truth on an advanced level. … It is sad when men and women who have been

Christians for years are found to be unaware of spiritual realities which should have great meaning, appeal, and power for them.[20]

A high level of spiritual maturity is commanded, expected and attainable (1 Corinthians 2:6; Philippians 3:15; Colossians 4:12). It comes through Bible study.

Benefits of Mary's Attentive Listening: Faith, Love and a Memorial

Attentive listening to the Word provides more than knowledge about God. It fosters love for Him with all one's heart, soul, strength and mind (Luke 10:27). Mary developed a deeper faith and love for Christ that showed in good works. We read about these in John 11-12.

Jesus made another trip to Bethany to raise dead Lazarus, the beloved brother of Mary and Martha (John 11:1-2, 11). As He came near the city, Jesus asked for Mary (vv. 28-30). One sister in my congregation pointed out, "Jesus craved Mary's fellowship!" She hurried to Him, fell at His feet, and expressed her faith in His power: "Lord, if you had been here, my brother would not have died" (v. 32). When Jesus saw her weeping, He groaned in the spirit and was troubled. Jesus wept (v. 35). Our compassionate Lord felt Mary's pain (Hebrews 4:15). He provided comfort for her as He always does for those who enjoy a special relationship with Him. This kind of relationship comes through listening to His Word.

After Jesus raised Lazarus, Mary demonstrated her love and gratitude (John 12:1-9). At the celebration dinner, she took a pound of expensive spikenard oil (worth 300 denarii, a year's wages, vv. 3, 5) and anointed Jesus' feet. She felt compelled to act, for her regular and attentive listening had given her unique insights into Jesus' mission. J. Ramsey Michaels notes,

> Only Mary anticipates and grasps the human significance of Jesus' words, and she displays her love accordingly. Though Mary has not understood that Jesus

is going away in glory to the "one who sent him," she at least understands that he is going away; and this for the time being is all that matters. Mary loves Jesus in his mortality, pouring out her love for him today because he may not be with her tomorrow. Here, if anywhere in the Bible, genuine human love is shown and defined.[21]

Mary accepted Jesus' impending death, unlike the disciples later in the upper room (John 13). They objected to the news that He was about to leave them and to His act of washing their feet (vv. 4-8, 36-37; 14:5). Mary, however, had symbolically prepared for His burial by washing – and anointing – His feet. Washing and anointing the bodies of loved ones was a custom Jews always performed before burial. John 19:40 explains that Nicodemus brought spices to anoint Jesus' body "as the custom of the Jews is to bury."

Mary showed her devotion in Jesus' living presence, and He defended her. When Judas complained that she "wasted" the fragrant oil and asked why it was not sold to help the poor, Jesus rebuked: "Don't stop her. It was right for her to save this perfume for today – the day for me to be prepared for burial. The poor people will always be with you. But you will not always have me" (John 12:7-8 ETRV).

Mark's account, which reveals that the dinner took place in the house of Simon the leper (Mark 14:3), gives a fuller description of Jesus' rebuke:

> Let her alone. Why do you trouble her? She has done a good work for Me. For you have the poor with you always, and whenever you wish you may do them good; but Me you do not have always. She has done what she could. She has come beforehand to anoint My body for burial. Assuredly, I say to you, wherever this gospel is preached in the whole world, what this woman has done will also be told as a memorial to her (Mark 14:6-9).

Jesus foretold that Mary of Bethany would be remembered. As Herbert Lockyer has beautifully stated, "The odor of Mary's loving service has filled the whole world." [22] Faithful attentiveness to His words created a legacy that still inspires readers. It fostered in Mary spiritual sensitivity and maturity. Lenski encouraged that we also choose "the one thing needful, the good part, i.e., the blessed, saving, soul-satisfying Word of Christ. Where this is chosen all else follows; where this is set aside and neglected all else is useless, empty, deceptive, vain." [23]

Is Bible study a priority in your life? We make time to do the things we really want to do. Kelly Weaver, the young mother mentioned at the beginning of this lesson, desperately wanted her twins to be healthy, so she diligently followed her doctor's instructions. Today she and Brandon remain committed to their children's physical and spiritual welfare. They are making the time and effort required (Deuteronomy 6:4-9).

Babies are supposed to grow, especially spiritually. The Great Physician has given us instructions in His Word. Mary of Bethany attentively listened while she sat at Jesus' feet. Through regular study of God's Word, we too can learn about our Lord and Savior, develop a special relationship with Him, and become transformed into blessed, holy women of God.

Reflection Questions

1. Satan tempts us with distractions. Name some things in your life that may seem virtuous but hinder attentive listening to God's Word.

2. Discuss the special relationship between Mary of Bethany and Jesus.

3. Scripture is God's revealed Word. Fischetto wrote, "When we abide in the Word of God daily through Bible study and meditation, our faith is transformed and grows deeper." [24] What scriptures help you most in your Christian journey?

4. Specific Bible verses guide us toward spiritually healthy works such as marriage, parenting, handling finances, etc. List other life principles discussed in Scripture.

5. The psalmist described the godly: "But his delight is in the law of the LORD, And in His law he meditates day and night" (Psalm 1:2). Share methods for Bible study that work for you.

Spiritual Exercise

Reading God's Word is more effective when we spend time meditating (concentrating, thinking) on it (Psalms 1:2; 63:6; 77:12; 119:15, 23, 48, 148; 143:5). Spend 10 minutes with Psalm 1, writing down your thoughts about every sentence. Ask questions like: What is the psalmist saying? How does it apply to me? Throughout the week, think about the passage. Write down any additional thoughts.

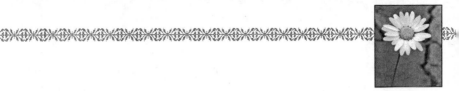

Chapter 2

Fervent Prayer
Hannah

1 Samuel 1:7-18

*L*esson 1 opened with a blessed event: the birth of babies. Some women can only rejoice with others on such occasions. Our congregation waited and prayed three years with Tammy, but she was unable to conceive. Meanwhile, she and her husband served the Lord by teaching Bible classes, visiting the sick and hosting church activities. In time, an unselfish birth mother chose them to adopt her beautiful baby girl, Abbey. As with the Weavers, our church family thanked God for blessing this good couple.

Scripture includes several barren women who prayed earnestly for children. In the days of Sarah, Rebekah and Rachel, this condition was considered a curse. Charles Carter explains, "No situation gave greater cause for anxious concern in patriarchal times, as is true among primitive people to the present, than the threat of childlessness. ... It was the first son who bore the family name, inherited the family possessions and continued the family after his father's death."[1] Being childless was especially painful for Jewish women; each wanted to be the one to bear the Messiah. Happily for the three Hebrew matriarchs, God opens wombs.

Hannah was another barren woman who lived generations later – after Abraham's descendants multiplied in Egypt, after they conquered the Promised Land, and near the end of the days of the judges. It was a dark time when Israel stopped wholly following God, and "everyone did what was right in his own eyes" (Judges 21:25). Hannah maintained a godly spirit even in this wicked environment and while enduring the burden of childlessness. First Samuel 1:5 says, "[T]he LORD had closed her womb."

The Scriptures' Message

Hannah desperately wanted a child. Elkanah, her husband, had children by his other wife (1 Samuel 1:2). Peninnah flaunted her motherhood before Hannah and made her "fret" (v. 6 KJV). The original word here means "to stir up inwardly," and that is where Hannah kept her intense frustration.[2] She did not respond to Peninnah's taunts with anger or vengeance. This holy woman suffered in silence until she could no longer hide her feelings.

The family had made its annual trip to worship in Shiloh. Elkanah gave a portion of the sacrificial meal to his wives and children. To Hannah he gave a double portion, which, sadly, prompted more vexation from Peninnah (1 Samuel 1:5-6). Hannah became so distraught that she could not enjoy the feast: "[S]he wept and did not eat" (v. 7). Elkanah's lack of understanding only added to her pain. He asked, "Hannah, why do you weep? Why do you not eat? And why is your heart grieved? Am I not better to you than ten sons?" (v. 8). One sister in my congregation made this observation:

> Hannah showed faith, patience, and courage in the face of discrimination and discouragement. She did not even complain about Peninnah to her husband. No whining or nagging. What strength! Elkanah did not know about her suffering for years. ... I'll bet he forgot their anniversary, too. Hannah could have blasted Peninnah, Elkanah and even Eli, who accused her of drunkenness. She blasted no one.

Despite overwhelming feelings of worthlessness and humiliation, this godly woman held her peace during the sacrificial meal. First Samuel 1:9 says, "Hannah arose after they had finished eating and drinking." Ronald S. Wallace, in *Hannah's Prayer and Its Answer*, asserts that she was "no longer content to wait indefinitely."[3] Her need for divine help was urgent. Perhaps she remembered Abraham's bargain with God concerning Sodom and Gomorrah (Genesis 18:23-32). Stanley Sayers beautifully states, "Prayer is that power which moves God to do those things He would not have done had we not prayed."[4] Hannah hoped to move God's heart.

With new resolve, she hurried to the temple to plead her case before God. Christians can still employ this avenue of hope: "Let us therefore come boldly to the throne of grace, that we may obtain mercy and find grace to help in time of need" (Hebrews 4:16). Confidence in prayer is essential, but Hannah's example also teaches us to pray with passion, humility and specificity.

Passion. Hannah's heart was filled with emotion. Scripture says she "poured out" her soul in prayer (1 Samuel 1:15). The Hebrew term for "poured out" literally means "the complete emptying of a container of its contents."[5] This type of prayer is called a "lament," that is, a prayer that gives voice to suffering caused by an enemy or rival and begs for help. God wants His children to cast all their cares on Him (1 Peter 5:7). After all, where can we go – where could Hannah go – but to the Lord? She passionately laid her cares at His feet.

Humility. Hannah acknowledged God's sovereignty and began her prayer with praise: "O LORD of hosts" (1 Samuel 1:11; "Lord All-Powerful" ETRV). She then presented her petition, asking Him to "remember" her. To "remember" meant to have mercy and to take action on a person's behalf. Hannah's plea was not unusual. Exodus 2:23-25 reveals that God remembered Israel when He heard their cry and delivered them from Egyptian bondage.

Jesus prayed for deliverance in Gethsemane: "[A]ll things are possible for You. Take this cup away from Me" (Mark 14:36). How many of us have cried, "Father, I know you can heal this disease" or "You have the power to make this problem go away"? It's okay to pray for deliverance from suffering. Alfred Lord Tennyson wrote, "More things are wrought by prayer than this world dreams of."[6] However, we must understand that sometimes God's answer is no. Jesus prayed, "[N]ot My will, but Yours, be done" (Luke 22:42). Hannah demonstrated this submissive attitude as she humbly referred to herself – three times – as "your maidservant" (1 Samuel 1:11).

Specificity. Hannah asked for a son. God wants us to be specific. In 2 Chronicles 1:7, He urged Solomon, "Ask! What shall I give you?" Jesus taught that "whatever things you ask in prayer, believing, you will receive" (Matthew 21:22). Hannah enveloped her specific request in a conditional oath: "[I]f You will indeed look on the affliction of Your maidservant and remember me, and not forget Your maidservant, but will give Your maidservant a male child, then I will give him to the LORD all the days of his life, and no razor shall come upon his head" (1 Samuel 1:11). She promised to give her son back to the Lord all the days of his life. Hannah wanted a child so badly that, as Carol Meyers states, she would "forgo the joys of raising him."[7]

Hannah's words were serious. The promise that no razor would come upon her son's head signaled a Nazirite vow. Bill Arnold, in the *NIV Application Commentary* on 1 and 2 Samuel, explains,

> The term *nazir* ("Nazirite") is defined in Numbers 6 where a man or woman can make a special vow of separation to Yahweh. The vow involves a period of time in which the Nazirite abstains from wine and other products of the vine, uses no razor on his or her head, and avoids contact with dead bodies. ... Numbers 6 prescribed a ritual for terminating the vow. Interestingly, in the case of Samson (Judges 13) and Samuel, the vow does not appear to be temporary but permanent. Thus, Hannah is offering her unborn child as a permanent Nazirite, whose life will be wholly and exclusively God's.[8]

At the temple, Hannah prayed "in bitterness of soul" and "wept in anguish" (1 Samuel 1:10). Eli, the priest, noted from his seat by the door that Hannah "spoke in her heart; only her lips moved, but her voice was not heard" (v. 13). R. Payne Smith, in *The Pulpit Commentary*, suggests that "possibly silent prayer was something unusual." Because he was "unused then to such real prayer, Eli, as he marked the quivering lips, the prostrate form, the face flushed with earnestness, came to the coarse conclusion that she was drunken."[9] Because drinking was customary at sacrificial meals, his was an honest mistake.

Eli rebuked Hannah and told her to put away her wine (1 Samuel 1:14). She replied, "No, my lord, I am a woman of sorrowful spirit. I have drunk neither wine nor intoxicating drink, but have poured out my soul before the LORD" (v. 15). In essence, she told him, "I am not drunk; I am desperate!"[10] Notice Hannah's godly attitude. One sister of my congregation mused, "What if Hannah had turned on Eli in anger? She had certainly been mistreated. Would he have blessed her? Would God have answered her prayer?"

Hannah's persistence paid off. Eli assured her that God would grant her petition (1 Samuel 1:17). Being at peace, she "went her way and ate, and her face was no longer sad" (v. 18). This reminds me of a friend who received a negative medical report and went home, lay on her bed, and poured out her soul to God. She explained later that only after her empowering prayer did she find strength to continue her daily responsibilities. Hannah left the temple with renewed hope.

The Lord remembered Hannah. She conceived and bore a son named Samuel, explaining, "Because I have asked for him from the LORD" (1 Samuel 1:19-20). The name "Samuel" is made up of two words: *sem* (name) and *el* (God), designating "he over whom the name of God has been said," or more simply, "asked of God."[11]

Prayer involves more than merely making requests of God. It also should include praise and thanks. "Hannah's Song," her prayer of thanksgiving in 1 Samuel 2:1-10, began with rejoicing over the fact that God had blessed her (vv. 1-2), followed by acknowledgement that God exalts the humble, needy and even barren (vv. 4-8). Finally, Hannah praised God's care for the righteous, His judgment on the wicked, and His promise of the Messiah (vv. 9-10). Prayer is our means of conversation with God, and it is essential in our quest for spiritual maturity.

The Maturity-Building Discipline of Prayer

We learn from Hannah that prayer must be practiced with confidence, passion, humility and specificity. Biblical models also reveal that prayer should include certain important elements. The following mnemonic devices can help us remember them.

• The acronym ACTSS presents five elements found throughout Scripture: [12]

A doration (praise) – "Every day I will bless You, and I will praise Your name forever and ever" (Psalm 145:2).

C onfession (pardon) – "If we confess our sins, He is faithful and just to forgive us our sins and to cleanse us from all unrighteousness" (1 John 1:9).

T hanksgiving – "Let us come before His presence with thanksgiving: Let us shout joyfully to Him with psalms" (Psalm 95:2).

S upplication (petition) – "Be anxious for nothing, but in everything by prayer and supplication, with thanksgiving, let your requests be made known to God" (Philippians 4:6).

S ubmission (providence) – "And whatever we ask we receive from Him, because we keep His commandments and do those things that are pleasing in His sight" (1 John 3:22).

• The Lord's model prayer in Matthew 6 and Luke 11 presents elements that can be described as "the four P's":

Praise – "Our Father in heaven, Hallowed be Your name."
Petition – "Give us this day our daily bread."
Pardon – "And forgive us our debts, As we forgive our debtors."
Providence – "And do not lead us into temptation, But deliver us from the evil one."

• The following suggestions, adapted from Rosemary McKnight's book *I Love Me, I Love Me Not,* may help us make time for prayer:[13]

(1) *Set a specific time for prayer.* Choose times best for you. Wake up early to pray before daily pressures come. Talk to God just before drifting off to sleep. Pray before meals.

(2) *Use small amounts of time for prayer.* As in Bible study, take advantage of times when hands are busy but the mind is free. Quick requests, called "flash prayers" or "telegraph prayers," are good in sudden anxious moments, such as when we hear about an accident or a missing child; but persistent prayers like Hannah's are essential.

(3) *Organize a list for prayer.* A list helps us remember and pray specifically. Keep a small notebook in your purse, and list the sick, unsaved friends and family, church matters, personal requests, and so on. Marking off answered prayers builds faith and confidence in prayer.

(4) *Make a prayer rock to create a habit for prayer.* A ladies' class teacher gave each student a small rock wrapped in cloth and tied with a pretty ribbon. Attached at the knot was a piece of paper on which the following poem was written:

I'm your little prayer rock,
And this is what I'll do.
Just put me on your pillow
until the day is through;

Then turn back your covers
and climb into bed,
And WHACK! Your little prayer rock
will hit you on the head.

Then you will remember
as the day is through
To kneel and say your prayers
as you wanted to.

When you are finished,
just dump me on the floor;

I'll stay there through the night
to give you help once more.

When you get up the next morning,
CLUNK! I'll stub your toe;
So you will remember your morning
prayers before you go.

Put me back upon your pillow
when your bed is made,
And your clever little prayer rock
will continue in your aid.

Because your heavenly Father
cares and loves you so,
He wants you to remember
to talk to Him, you know.
                              – Author unknown

Regular prayer can be a life-changing, maturity-building habit. Why not begin today?

Benefits of Hannah's Prayer: Transformed Heart and History

Richard J. Foster, author of spiritual formation literature, suggests, "Prayer is the central avenue God uses to transform us." [14] Hannah developed spiritual maturity through her struggle and prayers for a child. Not only did she live amidst moral depravity, but her annual trek to Shiloh exposed her to corruption in the religious elite (Eli's sons). First Samuel 1:3 explains, "This man went up from his city yearly to worship and sacrifice to the LORD of hosts in Shiloh. Also the two sons of Eli, Hophni and Phinehas, the priests of the LORD, were there." They are described as "corrupt" [literally, as sons of Belial (Satan)]; "they did not know the LORD" (2:12). They intimidated worshipers and took portions of sacrifices for themselves. Their sins were "very great before the LORD" (1:3; 2:12-17).

Such wickedness must have grieved Hannah. How she must

have agonized over the fate of her nation and cried, "What can one woman do?" The providence of God was apparently working. Wallace suggests that Hannah – seeing the immorality around her – was "introduced to a sorrow more urgent than her own sense of rejection. ... She was given this burden of shame and concern, because he [God] was calling her into his service in this crisis."[15]

Hannah may have asked herself, "Have my prayers for a child sprung from selfish desire?" James explained that sometimes we do not receive because we ask amiss, that we may spend it on our own pleasures (James 4:3). The psalmist added, "If I regard iniquity in my heart, The Lord will not hear" (Psalm 66:18). Why had God not yet opened her womb? Was He waiting for a change of purpose in her request? Foster points out, "In prayer, real prayer, we begin to think God's thoughts after him: to desire the things he desires, to love the things he loves, to will the things he wills."[16]

Wallace further suggests that, as Hannah pondered the downward spiral of God's people, she may have been "challenged with burning anger," and as she realized there was something she could do, her commitment to God's service became a "turning point" in her life.[17] Hannah's prayer at Shiloh reflected a new focus, for it included an unselfish pledge: "If God blesses me with a child, I will use this gift to glorify Him." On this day she determined "to bear a child to be the man of God who could put things right."[18] And the Lord made this possible.

Hannah weaned Samuel and brought him to Shiloh. It must have been a bittersweet day – a mixture of joy and sadness – praising God for His generosity, yet placing her son into the hands of Eli, whose own parenting skills were obviously deficient. But Hannah kept her promise to God. She explained to Eli,

> Oh my lord! As your soul lives, my lord, I am the woman who stood by you here, praying to the LORD. For this child I prayed, and the LORD has granted me my petition which I asked of Him. Therefore I also

have lent him to the LORD; as long as he lives he shall be lent to the LORD (1 Samuel 1:26-28).

The following poem by Edgar Guest, has touched the hearts of other mothers who have given up a child to God:

A Child of Mine

I will lend you, for a little time
A child of mine, He said.
For you to love the while he lives
And mourn for when he's dead.

It may be six or seven years,
Or twenty-two or three.
But will you, 'til I call him back,
Take care of him for Me?

He'll bring his charms to gladden you,
And should his stay be brief,
You'll have his lovely memories
As solace for your grief.

I cannot promise he will stay
Since all from earth return.
But there are lessons taught down there
I want this child to learn.

I've looked the wide world over
In search for teachers true.
And from the throngs that crowd life's lanes,
I have selected you.

Now will you give him all your love,
Nor think the labor vain,
Nor hate Me when I come
To take him home again?

I fancied that I heard them say,
"Dear Lord, Thy will be done!"
For all the joys Thy child shall bring,
The risk of grief we'll run.

We'll shelter him with tenderness,
We'll love him while we may
And for the happiness we've known,
Forever grateful stay.

But should the angels call for him
Much sooner than we've planned,
We'll brave the bitter grief that comes
And try to understand.[19]

Because of Hannah's fervent prayer, her son became the leader who brought Israel back to God. Kenneth Mulzac points out that "it was during this particular visit to Shiloh that a series of events was launched that changed the course of Israelite history," for Samuel, the godly son born of Hannah's prayer, "eventually replaced Hophni and Phinehas (1 Samuel 2:34-35)."[20] Under Samuel's leadership, "[t]he people of Israel began to follow the Lord again" (7:2 ETRV).

"Hannah was willing to sacrifice her most treasured gift – the opportunity to mother her son," said one sister of my congregation. "But she knew her true gratification would be for him to be a blessed child of God." Such knowledge provides peace for parents. John wrote, "I have no greater joy than to hear that my children walk in truth" (3 John 1:4). What peace Hannah enjoyed in her old age! Because of her sacrifice, God blessed Hannah with five more children: three sons and two daughters (1 Samuel 2:21).

Such sacrifice is reflected in the heart of the birth mother who gave up little Abbey to ensure a Christian upbringing with Tammy and Cameron. Six years later it was reflected again in another mother who chose them to adopt a second child, Molly Grace. God still answers prayers. In various ways, He still fills the arms of those longing to have children. And like Hannah in her song of thanksgiving, His children still rejoice.

Discussion Questions

1. Describe the circumstances under which you have poured out your heart to God in the past. Do you know of times when friends have poured out their hearts to God, too? What were the results?

2. Why did God answer Hannah's prayer?

3. Discuss some of the deliberations Hannah may have had in giving up her child.

4. Compare our world to the period of the judges in which Hannah lived. What can one woman do today to effect some change in society?

5. Do you think Hannah would have accepted God's answer for a child if it had been no? Why or why not?

Spiritual Exercise

Write out a prayer that includes the biblical elements discussed in this lesson. Keep it in your Bible to use when asked to lead prayer in your ladies' group.

Chapter 3

Effectual Fasting
Esther

Esther 4:16

Loving church families share more than joys and sorrows; they share fellowship meals. Someone has jokingly said that the church is so well-known for potlucks, its religious symbol could be a casserole dish. Eating together is a wonderful church tradition that began in the first century (Acts 2). But as we emulate the "feasting" of early Christians, we may be ignoring another of their faith-building exercises: fasting.

"Fasting" is defined as "abstaining from something for a specific period." Many of us have abstained from food before medical tests or to lose weight. Physicians say it is good to rest the digestive system periodically. We do this at night; then we "break fast" in the morning.

A religious fast involves abstaining from food for spiritual purposes. Scripture presents people fasting in serious petition to God. David fasted when his child was deathly ill (2 Samuel 12:21). The Ninevites proclaimed a fast of repentance after Jonah's sermon (Jonah 3:5). King Jehoshaphat called for Israel to fast before battle (2 Chronicles 20:3). People in the New Testament also fasted (Matthew 17:21; Mark 9:29; Acts 10:30; 14:23; 1 Corinthians 7:5).

Three types of spiritual fasts exist.[1] Doing without both food and drink is called an "absolute fast." Paul neither ate nor drank for three days after encountering Jesus on the road to Damascus (Acts 9:9). Esther called for the same before approaching Ahasuerus (Esther 4:16). Abstaining only from food is called a "partial fast." Jesus ate nothing for 40 days before His wilderness temptation by Satan (Luke 4:2), but it does not say whether He went without water. Moses experienced the third type of fast when he went 40 days and nights without food or water on Mount Sinai (Deuteronomy 9:9). This is called a "supernatural fast" because God preserved him. Three days is about as long as the human body can go without water.

The Scriptures' Message

Esther, the Jewish orphan turned queen of Persia, asked her people to fast for her. She had a comfortable position in the royal family but was awakened to a need that threatened her security. She needed courage to intervene on behalf of her people.

Esther is introduced as Hadassah, the daughter of Abihail. She was raised by her cousin Mordecai. They remained in Persia after the Southern Kingdom was released from captivity:

> In Shushan the citadel, there was a certain Jew whose name was Mordecai the son of Jair, the son of Shimei, the son of Kish, a Benjamite. Kish had been carried away from Jerusalem with the captives who had been captured with Jeconiah king of Judah, whom Nebuchadnezzar the king of Babylon had carried away. And Mordecai had brought up Hadassah, that is, Esther, his uncle's daughter, for she had neither father nor mother. The young woman was lovely and beautiful. When her father and mother died, Mordecai took her as his own daughter (Esther 2:5-7).[2]

God's people had been taken captive to Babylon in 586 B.C. (2 Kings 25:8-11; 2 Chronicles 36:17-20). They became discouraged waiting for deliverance (Psalms 74; 79; 137). After Persian King

Cyrus overtook the Babylonians, he released the Jews to return to Jerusalem in 539 B.C. (2 Chronicles 36:22-23; Jeremiah 29:10; Isaiah 45:1).[3] At that time 42,360 Jews chose to go back to their homeland with Zerubbabel (Ezra 1-2). Others remained in Persia, having put down roots and being assimilated into its culture. It has been suggested that some Jews saw God as uninvolved and distant, and they failed to identify with Him and His future purposes.[4] This may describe Esther's contemporaries.

The book of Esther opens during the third year of Ahasuerus (Esther 1:1-3). This is believed to be the Hebrew name of Persian King Xerxes (Greek name), who ruled 486–465 B.C. Xerxes was the son of Darius I (king in the time of Daniel).[5] Esther 1 reveals that Ahasuerus banished his wife, Vashti, for refusing to parade her beauty before his guests (vv. 10-22). He then searched for a new queen among all the "beautiful young virgins" in the land (2:3). They were brought to the palace and pampered in a one-year purification process: six months with oil of myrrh and six with perfumes and cosmetics. Who wouldn't enjoy such beauty treatments? At the end of her year, each was taken to the king so he could "try her out in bed" and then returned the next morning to the concubine harem to await the king's decision (v. 14).[6]

Esther was among the girls brought to the palace (Esther 2:8). Perhaps this precipitated her name change from Hadassah: "Esther had not revealed her people or family; for Mordecai had charged her not to reveal it" (v. 10). She did not know God's special plan for her life. It was no coincidence that she pleased Hegai, keeper of the king's harem, and that she obtained "grace and favor" in the sight of Ahasuerus (v. 17). It should not be surprising that he loved her, set the royal crown upon her head, and made her queen. One scholar suggests that the term "favor" may imply "God had quietly paved the way for Esther's reception."[7]

God had placed Esther where He needed her. About four years later she would affect Israel's history (Esther 2:16; 3:7). Ahasuerus promoted an Agagite named Haman and commanded everyone to show him reverence. However, Mordecai refused to bow (vv. 1-2). This angered Haman, so he "sought to destroy all the

Jews who were throughout the whole kingdom of Ahasuerus –
the people of Mordecai" (v. 6). Esther still had not revealed her
ethnicity, so neither Ahasuerus nor Haman knew she was a Jew.
Haman suggested to the king:

> There is a certain people ... and they do not keep
> the king's laws. Therefore it is not fitting for the
> king to let them remain. If it pleases the king, let a
> decree be written that they be destroyed, and I will
> pay ten thousand talents of silver into the hands of
> those who do the work, to bring it into the king's
> treasuries (Esther 3:8-9).

Ahasuerus signed an edict to carry out Haman's scheme. The
plot was made public to kill "all the Jews, both young and old,
little children and women, in one day, on the thirteenth day of
the twelfth month" (Esther 3:13). Verse 15 reveals that the city
of Shushan was perplexed by this. When the Jews read the edict,
they mourned and fasted. They wept in sackcloth and ashes (4:3),
including Mordecai, who cried loudly at the king's gate. No one
was allowed to "enter the king's gate clothed with sackcloth"
(vv. 1-2). When Esther learned about Mordecai's actions, she
was "deeply distressed" (v. 4).

Some interesting traits are revealed about Esther. First, she continued hiding her identity as one of God's people, and it appears she
was uninvolved with them. As they wept and mourned, it seems
she was unaware of the king's edict (Esther 4:5-8). Is it possible for
a child of God to become so caught up in her career that she does
not know what is going on in God's family? We can assume that
Esther did not worship regularly with her people, join in their fellowships, or attend the weddings and baby showers. Yes, a person
can become so busy in a secular lifestyle that she is uninvolved with
her spiritual brothers and sisters. This seems to describe Esther.

Second, Esther seemed comfortable in her uninvolved state.
Her reaction to Mordecai's mourning is interesting. She did not
tell the first messenger to find out what was wrong; rather, she
simply "sent garments to clothe Mordecai and take his sackcloth

away" (Esther 4:4). Maybe she did not want to arouse suspicion that she was related to this disturber of the peace. Michael V. Fox offers an interesting suggestion:

> Perhaps she is afraid he is making waves; she has, after all, lived in secretiveness for several years. Her focus on superficials is to be expected of a young woman whose daily routine places overwhelming importance on her appearance, and whose excellence in that regard has brought her to what everyone around her views as the ultimate in feminine success.[8]

However, Esther's concern for Mordecai moved her to further action. When he refused the clothing, she sent Hathach, her attending eunuch, to find out the problem. Maybe she hoped to resolve it quickly and quietly. But Esther 4:7-8 reveals,

> And Mordecai told him of all that had happened to him, and the sum of money that Haman had promised to pay into the king's treasuries to destroy the Jews. He also gave him a copy of the written decree for their destruction, which was given at Shushan, that he might show it to Esther and explain it to her, and that he might command her to go in to the king to make supplication to him and plead before him for her people.

Mordecai advised Esther that because she was in a position of influence, she must intervene.

Esther's response revealed a third weakness in herself: She balked. It appears that she cared more about herself than her people. If she had been passionately concerned about them, she would have been eager to speak to the king. A friend in my congregation made this thoughtful application: "Would I risk my secure position in life for the will of God?"

If Esther did what Mordecai asked, she might follow Vashti into banishment or, more likely, lose her life. It was against the law to enter the king's presence without invitation.[9] Esther sent word to Mordecai:

All the king's servants and the people of the king's provinces know that any man or woman who goes into the inner court to the king, who has not been called, he has but one law: put all to death, except the one to whom the king holds out the golden scepter, that he may live. Yet I myself have not been called to go in to the king these thirty days (Esther 4:11).

Why was Esther uninvolved with God's people, comfortable in that state, and unwilling to risk her life to help? Opinions vary. Regarding the fact that some Jews remained in Persia after Cyrus released them, Dave Bland offers, "It may be that in becoming indifferent toward the restoration, they began to wonder if Yahweh, after these many years of captivity, was still present in their lives." [10] Perhaps Mordecai felt this way and was not diligent in modeling faith before Esther. We know that Nehemiah, the cupbearer to Xerxes' son King Artexerxes 35 to 40 years later, confessed Israel's religious passivity (Nehemiah 1:5-7).

Such indifference may explain why God's name is conspicuously absent in the book of Esther. Forrest S. Weiland proposes,

The tension caused by silence about God's involvement and the apparent overruling of events (foiling the plot) moves the reader to ask, if God was involved, why did He not show up in the story? A possible answer is that Mordecai's desire to keep Esther's Jewishness secret (Esther 2:10, 20) may reflect an attitude of the postexilic Jews who declined to return to the land of Israel. If these Jews sought deliverance but not necessarily the Deliverer, then God may have honored their desire by concealing His participation in the events. [11]

If Mordecai had such an attitude, this would explain why he may not have encouraged Esther's adherence to God's laws. She committed fornication with the pagan king and married outside God's family (Exodus 20:14; Deuteronomy 7:1-3). Iain Duguid asserts, "[O]n Mordecai's advice, she lived such an assimilated lifestyle that even her nearest companions were unaware of her

Jewishness, which must have meant ignoring virtually all of the Mosaic commandments ([Esther] 2:10)."[12] And, according to Leland Ryken, it is not far-fetched to conclude that Esther had "compromised her religious principles when she fit so well into the Persian court."[13] Like me, you may have viewed Esther only as a courageous heroine. She was – but not at first. Scripture presents her spiritual maturity as a process.

Some point out the fact that Esther was young, immature and simply did as she was told. Fox observes, "Of course, she had no choice ... [T]he author seeks to convey the insignificance of her will and mind at this stage. Esther is putty – not because of any personality flaw, but because of age and situation. Nothing has ever challenged her to be anything more."[14] Until Haman's threat to her people, Esther's faith had not been tested. Karen Jobes notes that this crisis became a "defining moment" in which she was "forced to choose between identifying herself with God's covenant people or continuing to live as a pagan in the king's court."[15] How many of us recognize and choose wisely in such defining moments?

If Esther was religiously passive at her coronation, she did not remain so. She had not identified with her people in four years, and, therefore, it did not occur to her that she would be included in the murderous edict. Mordecai gave Esther a wake-up call:

> Esther, don't think that just because you live in the king's house you will be the only Jew to escape. If you keep quiet now, help and freedom for the Jews will come from another place. But you and your father's family will all die. And who knows, maybe you have been chosen to be the queen for such a time as this? (Esther 4:13-14 ETRV).

It was time for Esther to acknowledge her spiritual roots and act on behalf of her people. But she needed support. Perhaps she remembered God's mighty works in Israel's history. Her ancestors had "fasted at times of mourning and national repentance ... when they needed strength or mercy to persevere and when they wanted a word from God."[16] Esther called for an absolute fast by urging Mordecai, "Go, gather all the Jews who are present in Shushan, and fast for me; neither eat nor drink for three days, night or day. My maids and I will fast likewise. And so I will go to the king, which is against the law; and if I perish, I perish!" (Esther 4:16). Esther needed help in this life-or-death decision.

In Scripture, fasting is usually accompanied by prayer. But prayer is not mentioned in the book of Esther. Bland suggests that the "deliberate avoidance of religious language … serves to catch the attention of a people who had been captive for so long, to remind them that Yahweh is still present in their lives."[17] Interestingly, Nehemiah fasted and prayed in the same palace before petitioning King Artexerxes about rebuilding the walls of Jerusalem. He wrote, "I sat down and wept, and mourned for many days; I was fasting and praying before the God of heaven" (Nehemiah 1:4). Did Esther bow her helpless soul before God's throne as she sought courage to go before her husband? William E. Burrows has beautifully stated this possibility:

> When the third day came she put on her royal apparel and did not appear unto men to fast; but meanwhile there was "another King" to whom she could go without delay, with whom she could remain longer, and to whom she could pour out all her heart. The mere force of contrast with the exclusive monarch of Persia brings up comforting and tender thoughts of the Lord Jesus, who does not debar from his presence the weary and heavy-laden, but bids them come; who has chosen the contrite heart as his earthly dwelling-place; who proclaims it as the glory of his home above that there he shall wipe away all tears.[18]

Ahasuerus accepted Esther's entrance. God was in control: "The king's heart is in the hand of the LORD, Like the rivers of water; He turns it wherever He wishes" (Proverbs 21:1). The king attended Esther's private dinner in which she revealed her identity and pleaded for the Jews. He proclaimed a new edict, allowing them to defend themselves (Esther 8:11).

The Maturity-Building Discipline of Fasting

Is fasting required today? It was practiced by early Christians. R.D. Linder has explained, "Jewish Christians apparently followed the Jewish custom of fasting and prayer on Mondays and Thursdays until around the end of the first century when Wednesdays and Fridays were observed."[19] For some, like the arrogant Pharisee in the temple, fasting had degenerated into a ritual for righteous appearance (Luke 18:10-14). In the Sermon on the Mount, Jesus warned against such ostentation and gave instructions for the three pillars of piety: when you give, when you pray, and when you fast (Matthew 6:2, 5, 16). The fourth-century theologian Augustine wrote, "Do you wish your prayer to fly toward God? Give it two wings: fasting and almsgiving."[20]

However, Scripture never specifically commands fasting. In fact, it presents early Christians voluntarily fasting "during special times of seeking God's guidance: for specific major decisions, for strength during extraordinary circumstances, for repentance, etc." (Acts 13:2-3; 14:23).[21] Notice that the Jewish widow Anna worshiped in the temple "with fastings and prayers night and day" (Luke 2:36-37); but Christian widows were required to continue only "in supplications and prayers night and day" (1 Timothy 5:5).

Still, it seems that Jesus assumed His followers would fast. When asked why His disciples did not fast, Jesus explained that although they did not fast regularly, the day would come when they would need fasts to strengthen themselves after He was gone (Matthew 9:15). Fasting helps us draw closer to God. It reminds us that we are sustained by His Word and not by earthly bread (4:4).

Fasting offers spiritual blessings, but there are physical benefits, too. Medical journals note positive results of supervised fasting for detoxifying the body and in treating obesity, diabetes, cardiovascular disease, autoimmune disorders, skin disease, gastrointestinal disease, arthritis and allergies.[22] Physicians say fasting is safe for one to three days without medical supervision if one is healthy (not a diabetic) and not pregnant or breast-feeding. You should consult a physician or nutritionist regarding longer periods of fasting. If you decide you would like to try fasting, here are some tips to make the experience safe:

TIPS FOR SAFE FASTING

(1) Try a partial 24-hour fast, drinking only fresh fruit juices. Fasting from lunch to lunch requires missing only two meals. Do this once a week for several weeks.

(2) After a few weeks, try a normal 24-hour fast, drinking only pure water. Richard Foster points out that hunger pangs are only signals your stomach has been trained to give at certain times. Ignore them. Sip a glass of water, and they will subside. [23]

(3) If short fasts work well, you may try a 36-hour fast, then a three- to seven-day fast. Read literature about fasting to understand the body's reaction to each phase of this process. Use caution and consult a physician. An informational report from Shaklee products states, [24]

> In the fasting state, the body undergoes metabolic changes to conserve energy. Early in fasting, the body manufactures glucose and releases stores of it from the liver. After a few days, the body releases triglycerides from the fat cells, and they are used for energy production. Body metabolism slows down to about 75 percent of normal rate. So you need plenty of rest and no vigorous exercise while fasting.

(4) Begin a fast by eating light meals focusing on raw fruits and raw and steamed vegetables. Drink plenty of liquids: water, if on a strict fast, and nonacidic juices and herbal teas if on a modified fast. After the fast, ease back into solid food with light meals of fruits and vegetables. Too much food may be uncomfortable.

As you fast, let hunger pangs remind you to find spiritual nourishment in God's Word. Adele Ahlberg Calhoun explains that fasting "opens us up to intentionally seeking God's will and grace in a way that goes beyond normal habits of worship and prayer." [25]

Benefits of Esther's Fast: Transformed Heart and History

Esther's courageous act demonstrates spiritual growth. Ryken described the process: "This beautiful young woman with a weak character becomes transformed into a person with heroic moral stature and political skill."[26] The fast moved Israel, notes Weiland, "from an attitude of estrangement and indifference in their relationship to Yahweh to one of dynamic faith in Him, amazement at His providential working, and gratitude for His care."[27] We see evidence of this as Ezra led a second group back to Jerusalem in 458 B.C. (Ezra 7:1-10) and as Nehemiah's third wave rebuilt the walls and repopulated the city in 444 B.C. (Nehemiah 7:6ff).

Three days of fasting helped give Esther courage. What an example she provides for us. Lottie Beth Hobbs wrote that Esther "proved how powerful one life can be when it is devoted to the service of the Lord."[28] She became memorialized in the annual Jewish Feast of Purim:

> It was established as an ordinance by edicts from Esther and Mordecai (Esther 9:20-22, 29-32), not from God. In it the Jews, both far and near, bound themselves to feast, rejoice, and give presents to one another and gifts to the poor, remembering Hainan's plot and the king's intervention to deliver them (vv. 24-25). ... Purim challenges its observers to see beyond the visible and recognize the redemptive hand of God in the hidden workings of history.[29]

Other nations have received God's help through prayer and fasting. Foster shares this example:

> When a sufficient number of people rightly understand what is involved, national calls to prayer and fasting can also have beneficial results. The king of Britain called for a day of solemn prayer and fasting because of a threatened invasion by the French in 1756. On

February 6 John Wesley recorded in his journal, "The fast day was a glorious day, such as London has scarce seen since the Restoration. Every church in the city was more than full, and a solemn seriousness sat on every face. Surely God heareth prayer, and there will yet be a lengthening of our tranquility." In a footnote he wrote, "Humility was turned into national rejoicing for the threatened invasion by the French was averted."[30]

The practice of fasting also can help us "refocus our attention on what really matters in life – a relationship with God."[31] Perhaps today, Christians might gather, fast, and pray for the needs of our people, our church and our nation, maybe even in place of some fellowship meals. Let us emulate the "feasting" of first-century Christians by engaging in the faith-building discipline that strengthened them: fasting.

Reflection Questions

1. Compare indications of Esther's spiritual maturity level before and after Mordecai's wake-up call.

2. Point out evidence of God's providence in the book of Esther.

3. Name some risks we face in life (home, career) when we stand up for what is right. How should we handle them?

4. Discuss some physical benefits of fasting.

5. Discuss some spiritual benefits of fasting.

Spiritual Exercise

Consider engaging in a "partial" fast (from lunch to lunch, missing only two meals). Spend these mealtimes in Bible study and prayer, and notice the physical and spiritual benefits you receive. Write about your experience.

Chapter 4

Humble Submission
Mary of Nazareth

Luke 1-26-55

*I*n order to open this lesson with a contemporary model, I looked for mothers with sons in ministry. There are many in my geographic area, including myself. Those I interviewed expressed pride in their children. Some revealed that although they had emphasized evangelism in the home, they were surprised when their sons became preachers. I am proud of my sons but not surprised. Since their births, my prayer was that all four would teach others. Two preach from the pulpit, but all have privately taught lost souls. This was the mission of Jesus (Luke 19:10).

When Mary of Nazareth was told she would bear the Savior of the world, was she surprised? Yes! Was she proud? According to Scripture, she was humble. The angel told her, "[Y]ou will conceive in your womb and bring forth a Son, and shall call His name JESUS" (Luke 1:31). And in true submission, Mary responded, "Behold the maidservant of the Lord! Let it be to me according to your word" (v. 38). She was open to God's will.

God chose Mary for a special task – a blessing that other Jewish women had coveted for centuries: the privilege to bear the promised Messiah. By the world's standards, this ordinary unwed teenage girl was an unlikely choice. You see, the world honors those who rate high on the social ladder, but God, who sees not as man sees (1 Samuel 16:7), prefers an inverted scale. He honors the lowly. This is a theme consistently running through Luke's gospel: the proud brought low and the lowly exalted; the self-righteous debased and the humble praised; and the rich impoverished while the poor are blessed.

Christ's birth was no exception. Luke 1:26-38 describes the supernatural conception of God's Son, a concept many still reject. In the birth story, some had honorable backgrounds: Elizabeth, Mary's cousin, was from the distinguished "daughters of Aaron"; Zechariah was a priest "of the division of Abijah"; and Joseph, Mary's fiancé, was "of the house of David" (vv. 5, 27). But Mary is simply described as "a virgin betrothed" (v. 27). She had no accolades of wealth or position. Joel B. Green writes,

> The stature of important persons in Luke-Acts is com-municated by special note of their pedigree, both kin and clan, thus extending the honor and identity of the ancestors to the contemporary individual. ... This is true of Elizabeth, Zechariah, and Joseph; what of Mary? That is, why not Mary?[1]

Mary had no noble pedigree. She was not from a respectable Judean city. Nazareth was in Galilee, originally *Gelil ha-goyim* ("district of the pagans"), also called "place of despised Gentiles." Its poor reputation is evident in Nathaniel's question, "Can any-thing good come out of Nazareth?" (John 1:46). Yet God knew Mary's heart, the kind we must have in order to fully serve Him. Darrell L. Bock notes, "Mary reflects the person whom God un-expectedly chooses to use. She brings no outstanding credentials to the task and lives on the edge of the nation. She brings noth-ing on her résumé other than her availability and willingness to serve."[2] How wonderful that no matter our background, each of us can find a place in God's kingdom.

The Scriptures' Message

Let's review Mary's visit by the angel Gabriel. He began God's message (termed "the Annunciation"): "Rejoice, highly favored one, the Lord is with you" (Luke 1:28). What a privilege! Esther had been honored by a Persian king, but Mary was favored by God Himself! Of course, she was awe-struck at the presence of His messenger. Therefore, Gabriel urged, "Do not be afraid, Mary, for you have found favor with God" (v. 30).

Raymond Brown suggests that the aorist verb *eures* ("have found") is noteworthy because Mary had found favor with God long before this point:

> The one whom God has chosen for the conception of his Son is one who has already enjoyed his grace by the way she has lived. Her discipleship, as we shall see, comes into being when she says yes to God's will about Jesus; but such readiness is possible for her because by God's grace she has said yes to him before. Thus Mary's discipleship does not exhibit conversion but consistency.[3]

Her love for God had developed early in life and spurred continual obedience to His will. Now as a teenager she was called into this special service, to bear the Son of God.

Gabriel confirmed the child's identity with the following description: "He will be great, and will be called the Son of the Highest; and the Lord God will give Him the throne of His father David. And He will reign over the house of Jacob forever, and of His kingdom there will be no end" (Luke 1:32-33).

Mary did not doubt the angel. Unlike Zechariah's response, "How can I be sure of this?" (Luke 1:18 NIV), she asked, "How will this be ... since I am a virgin?" (v. 34). Gabriel revealed how this unique conception would took place: "The Holy Spirit will come upon you, and the power of the Highest will overshadow you; therefore, also, that Holy One who is to be born will be called the Son of God" (v. 35). Interestingly, no mention had been made of the Holy Spirit operating among God's people for centuries; here in the "fullness of the time" (Galatians 4:4), its miraculous work was performed in this godly young woman. Brown beautifully writes, "Mary's conception involves a divine creative action without human intercourse; it is the work of the overshadowing Spirit, that same Spirit that hovered at the creation of the world when all was void (Genesis 1:2)."[4]

To prove God's power over conception, the angel informed Mary that her "barren," elderly cousin, Elizabeth, was six months' pregnant. He proclaimed, "For with God nothing will be impossible" (Luke 1:36-37). A similar response was given in the Old Testament to confirm Sarah's conception: "Is anything too hard for the LORD?" (Genesis 18:14).

Without hesitation, Mary pledged unconditional submission to God's plan. Did she worry about what others would think? Surely, an unwed pregnancy would affect her social position and relationships. Betrothal in ancient times was an official engagement, as legally binding as marriage.[5] Infidelity was a capital offense, and Mary could have been stoned to death (Deuteronomy 22:23-24). Joseph planned to divorce his pregnant fiancée privately until God sent an angel to explain her situation (Matthew 1:19-20).

The Lord's promise to be with her was enough for Mary (Luke 1:28). Bravely, she surely endured whispers at the market and condemning looks at worship. We cannot imagine the shame and rejection she must have suffered. As Bock has commented on Mary's plight:

> In ancient culture, virginity was an honored state, a badge of self-control and moral faithfulness. Mary would appear to many to have conceived a child out of wedlock. Her explanation of a divine conception would be hard to swallow (cf. Matthew 1:18-25). ... Our culture unfortunately accepts sexual experience before wedlock as almost a given. Thus it is hard to appreciate the walk of faith Mary is asked to take here. In the midst of it all, however, what overwhelms her is not the "risk" of appearance, with its potential risk

to her reputation, but the joy of serving and being involved with God.[6]

Mary's humble submission is revealed in her self-description as "maidservant" (Luke 1:38). The term is translated from the Greek word *doulos*, meaning "slave." Mary was a true servant. Richard Foster contrasts choosing to serve and choosing to be a servant, suggesting that when we decide whom and when we will serve, we are in charge, but when we choose to be a servant, we give up that right.[7] Mary served God through unconditional submission. Ancient philosopher Augustine offered, "Mary first conceived Christ in her heart by faith, before she conceived in the womb."[8]

This brings up a significant concept in biblical submission: human free-moral agency. H.D.M. Spence, in *The Pulpit Commentary*, suggests that God waited for Mary's acceptance of His plan, for Gabriel's message was in the future tense: "You will conceive" (Luke 1:31). He quoted Frederic Louis Godet:

> "God's message," writes Godet, "by the mouth of the angel was not a command. The part Mary had to fulfill made no demands on her. It only remained, therefore, for Mary to consent to the consequences of the Divine offer. She gives this consent in a word at once simple and sublime, which involved the most extraordinary act of faith that a woman ever consented to accomplish. Mary accepts the sacrifice of that which is dearer to a young maiden than her very life, and thereby becomes pre-eminently the heroine of Israel, the ideal daughter of Zion."[9]

Of course, God knew Mary's heart and that she would accept even before He sent Gabriel.

God often made requests of people in Scripture. He instructed Abraham to leave his home for an unknown destination (Genesis 12:1-4). The prophet Hosea was directed to marry a prostitute (Hosea 1:2). Here, Mary is told, "[Y]ou will conceive in your womb and bring forth a Son" (Luke 1:31). Could these individuals have refused? Not without consequences. "This shows that we aren't

God's puppets, but that those who are faithful will follow Him and what He commands without asking questions or knowing why," says a sister of my congregation. "If Mary could bear the Messiah, knowing she will be talked about, I don't think it is too much for us to do what He asks."

Paul explained in 1 Corinthians 6:19 that we are not our own; that is, we do not belong to ourselves. We were bought with a price; therefore, we belong to Him. But God wants voluntary submissive service. Mary understood this. Bock explains, "She knows she is God's servant, so she will allow God to work through her as he wills. He can place her in whatever difficult circumstances he desires, for she knows that God is with her." [10] What a model for us today!

The Maturity-Building
Discipline of Submission

Mary of Nazareth was the epitome of submission. This discipline is probably the most unpopular and misunderstood. The world calls submission "repugnant," and some suggest it conjures up "images of becoming a doormat, a weak-willed nonentity or a brainwashed cult follower." [11] But biblical submission is not blind obedience. It is voluntarily placing oneself under the will of a recognized authority. Warren W. Wiersbe, in his book *Be Faithful*, explains the meaning of the Greek root word:

> It literally means "to rank under." Anyone who has served in the armed forces knows that "rank" has to do with order and authority, not with value or ability. A colonel is higher in rank than a private, but that does not necessarily mean that the colonel is a better man than the private. It only means that the colonel has a higher rank and, therefore, more authority. [12]

Who would view the private as a brainwashed cult follower? He voluntarily submits to the recognized authority. If privates disobeyed authority on the battlefield, imagine the chaos! Remember Hannah's world, when Israel disregarded God's authority and "everyone did what was right in his own eyes" (Judges 21:25). Disrespect for authority always produces a chaotic, lawless environment.

Mary acknowledged God's sovereignty. How different our world would be if His authority was so recognized today (1 Chronicles 29:11)! Bock concurs:

> Humility is the natural product of reflection about who God is. In the ancient world, relationship with God was not a casual affair, as if God were a friendly neighbor. Rather, it was seen as an honor, and it called for a deep sense of respect, much like a person might respond to hosting a famous dignitary. After all, he is the Creator, who is responsible for our being a part of his creation. So much awe was reserved for God in Judaism that they discussed in detail how he should be approached in worship at the temple, even giving the precise route the priests should take in approaching him.[13]

God does not force obedience. He wants us to recognize that He knows best. Everything He commands us to do is good for us. Everything He tells us to avoid is harmful. Godly submission brings blessings because, as Adele Calhoun notes, it is rooted in "God's good and loving intentions" for us.[14]

For our good, God ordained authoritative roles on earth. An orderly society can be maintained only when we submit to leadership in the government, work, church and home.

• *Government.* Legal systems are set up to establish law, carry out justice and keep peace. Paul described our responsibility:

> Let every soul be subject to the governing authorities. For there is no authority except from God, and the authorities that exist are appointed by God. Therefore whoever resists the authority resists the ordinance of God, and those who resist will bring judgment on themselves. For rulers are not a terror to good works, but to evil. Do you want to be unafraid of the authority? Do what is good, and you will have praise from the same (Romans 13:1-3).

Law-abiding citizens recognize the authority of God's "ministers" (Romans 13:6). But this does not include blind obedience. If civil law conflicts with biblical commands, "[w]e ought to obey God rather than men" (Acts 5:29). Some today are forced to choose between civil law and losing their jobs. Solomon wrote, "When the righteous are in authority, the people rejoice; But when a wicked man rules, the people groan" (Proverb 29:2). Therefore, let us heed Paul's admonition to "pray for kings and for all people who have authority (power). Pray for those leaders so that we can have quiet and peaceful lives" (1 Timothy 2:2 ETRV).

• **Work.** Employees should submit to their employer's authority. Schools operate smoothly when teachers follow the principal's instructions. Hospitals are more efficient when doctors respect the administration's directives. Chaos results when workers disregard authority. Paul's instructions to servants easily apply in the workplace:

> Slaves [servants, KJV], obey your masters here on earth. Obey with fear and respect. And do that with a heart that is true, the same as you obey Christ. You must do more than just obey your masters to please them while they are watching you. You must obey them like you are obeying Christ. With all your heart you must do what God wants. Do your work, and be happy to do it. Work like you are serving the Lord, not like you are serving only men (Ephesians 6:5-7).

The text instructs those in authority to submit to God's laws by treating their workers right (v. 9).

• **Church.** The Lord also designed church leadership. Christians are told how to respond to elders: "Obey your leaders and be under their authority. Those men are responsible for you. So they are always watching to protect your souls. Obey those men so that they will do this work with joy, not sadness. It will not help you to make their work hard" (Hebrews 13:17 ETRV). These shepherds are not to dominate ("lord it over") the congregation, but to be gentle examples (1 Peter 5:1-4). They are accountable to

Christ. Godly church leadership was established for our benefit.
• *Home.* Submission to authority is learned in the home. Paul wrote, "Children, obey your parents in the Lord, for this is right" (Ephesians 6:1). Children learn respect by watching mothers heed Ephesians 5:22-23: "Wives, submit to your own husbands, as to the Lord. For the husband is head of the wife, as also Christ is head of the church." Few disagree that the church should follow Christ. He leads – not with force, but with love, as husbands are commanded to do (5:25-33). Wives are "joint-heirs" to be honored (1 Peter 3:7 ASV). A wife should submit voluntarily to authority in the home as part of her love for the Lord. This principle, established at creation (Genesis 3:16), was designed by God for order and unity.[15]

Christians also must be willing to submit to each another (Ephesians 5:21). Although some demand their rights, Jesus said that in order to follow Him, we must deny ourselves (Mark 8:34). This explains how Mary was able to overcome the whispers, the rejection and, later, the piercing of her soul (Luke 2:35). H.D.M. Spence has observed,

> The lot proposed to her would bring probably in its wake unknown sufferings as well as untold blessedness. We may with all reverence think Mary already feeling the first piercings in her heart of that sharp sword which was one day to wound so deeply the mother of sorrows; yet in spite of all this, in full view of the present woe, which submission to the Divine will would forthwith bring upon her, with an unknown future of sorrow in the background, Mary submitted herself of her own free will to what she felt was the will and wish of her God.[16]

God has a plan for each of us (Jeremiah 29:11). Through true biblical submission we allow His agenda to shape our choices.[17] Mary accepted the privilege for which she was chosen by God. She humbled herself and, as promised (Luke 14:11), she was exalted. As Herbert Lockyer describes it, "The Holy Spirit, by His gentle operation, took Deity and humanity and fused them together and formed the love-knot between our Lord's two natures [physical and spiritual] within Mary's being."[18]

Benefits of Mary's Submission: An Exalted Handmaid and a Savior's Birth

After Gabriel appeared to her, Mary made a four-day journey to visit her cousin Elizabeth. At Mary's greeting, Elizabeth felt her own baby leap in her womb. She was filled with the Holy Spirit and cried, "Blessed are you among women, and blessed is the fruit of your womb!" (Luke 1:42). Millions have honored Mary since that day. Although some religions exalt Mary by holding to a "dogmatic and sentimental exaggeration of her eminence," others have simply made her name one of the most popular in Christian lands.[19] The name "Mary" is related to the Hebrew "Miriam" and "Marah," root forms of "bitterness." This is an attitude that some in Mary's situation might have developed.

Elizabeth called Mary "the mother of my Lord" (Luke 1:43). Spence, suggesting that the Spirit opened her eyes to see that Mary carried the coming Messiah, writes:

> Think what must have been the feeling of the two – the one finding herself the chosen out of all the thousands of Israel, after so many centuries of weary waiting, to be the mother of the Messiah; the other, long after any reasonable hope of any offspring at all had faded away, to be the mother of Messiah's chosen friend, his herald, and his preacher, the mighty forerunner of the King of whom the prophets had written![20]

After sharing her joyous news, Mary burst into a thanksgiving song (Luke 1:46-55). This extemporaneous ode is well-known by its Latin name, "Magnificat." Lockyer calls it "one of the choicest gems of Hebrew poetry."[21] The Magnificat may be divided into two parts: Mary's personal praise for her specific situation (vv. 46-49) and a hymn of praise for God's general activity (vv. 50-55).[22] Read and compare this with the opening of Hannah's song (1 Samuel 2:1-2).

After nine months, Mary "brought forth her firstborn Son ... a Savior, who is Christ the Lord" (Luke 2:7, 11). She proceeded to be a devoted mother to Jesus for 30 years, giving Him life, a home, a sense of God's presence, and an example of obedience to His will.[23]

Jesus imitated his mother's humble submission. Just as Mary accepted the stigma on her reputation to bear Him, this son submitted to a life of rejection and the old rugged cross. He denied Himself and gave up His rights for the needs of a lost world. He emptied Himself, took the form of a servant, and humbled Himself, becoming obedient, even unto death on the cross (Philippians 2:7-8). Hebrews 5:8-9 adds that the Son of God became perfect through His obedience and suffering. Such submission produces spiritual maturity in Christians today (James 1:2-4).

From Mary of Nazareth we learn that God blesses submissive hearts. This ordinary teenage girl was "favored" by God. She did not describe herself as proud but as a humble "maidservant." Wiersbe observes:

> Mary's response reveals her humility and honesty before God. She certainly never expected to see an angel and receive special favors from heaven. There was nothing unique about her that such things should happen. If she had been different from other Jewish girls, as some theologians claim she was, then she might have said, "Well, it's about time! I've been expecting you!" No, all of this was a surprise to her.[24]

As Lockyer beautifully concludes, "The gentle and lowly Mary of Nazareth was the Father's choice as the mother of His beloved Son, and that she herself was overwhelmed at God's condescending grace in choosing her is evident from her song of praise in which she magnified Him for regarding her lowly estate, and in exalting her."[25] The Bible does not describe Mary as proud. But we may assume she was very pleased and grateful that her son, the Savior of the world, came to seek and save the lost. And so must we be!

Reflection Questions

1. With Mary's humble background in mind, discuss requirements for service in God's kingdom.

2. Name some long-term advantages of submitting to God's will early in one's life, rather than later.

3. Discuss the significance of the phrase "the Lord is with you" for Mary's life.

4. In what life situations do you find yourself choosing to be a servant, rather than choosing to serve?

5. Discuss qualities in Mary that may have influenced Jesus' character.

Spiritual Exercise

Read the biblical commands presented in this lesson for submission to government, work, church and home. Consider which you find the most difficult. Consider your obstacles and what you can do to better follow God's directive.

Chapter 5

Loving Service
Dorcas

Acts 9:36-42

An elder of a small rural church told the custodian about a dead spider in the ladies room. His wife had noticed it every Sunday for weeks and wanted it removed. This was a missed opportunity for service! Of course, spider disposal doesn't compare with feeding the hungry and visiting the sick, but it certainly fits a definition of true service: to minister when there is a need.

Most congregations have some truly servant-hearted members. In our congregation was Mabel Moss, a Christian who saw needs and acted. She noticed that one of our men, who suffered from nerve damage, had difficulty with his winter coat. It was difficult for him to get his arms in the sleeves, and the cuffs hurt his wrists. Mabel did not contact the elders or discuss this problem with the ladies class. She simply made him a warm, loosely fitting coat. This fine lady went to her reward in 2006. But when the weather turns cold and we see that blue, open-sleeved jacket still providing warmth and comfort for our brother, we remember Mabel and the works that followed her (Revelation 14:13).

The Scriptures' Message

The book of Acts presents accounts of Christian servanthood. In Chapter 2 we read about the Jerusalem saints who fellowshiped daily and attended to each others' needs (Acts 2:42-47). Jon M. Walton calls the entire document "a yearbook of the church" in which Luke lingers with particular interest over the photo of one special lady.[1]

Her Aramaic name was Tabitha, meaning "gazelle: an emblem of grace and beauty."[2] The Greeks called her Dorcas. She lived in Joppa (now Jaffa, a suburb of Tel-Aviv), a seaport about 35 miles northwest of Jerusalem (Acts 9:36). This is the city where Jonah boarded a ship to avoid preaching to Nineveh (Jonah 1:3). In the first century, soon after Peter's Pentecost sermon, Philip preached the gospel in all the cities between Azotus and Caesarea, including Joppa (Acts 8:40). A congregation was established there, and Dorcas became an active member.

Luke describes her as a "disciple" (Acts 9:36). The feminine form of this term, *mathetria* ("pupil, follower"), occurs only here in Scripture. We know that Dorcas followed the example of Jesus; she "went about doing good" (10:38), for she was "full of good works and charitable deeds" (9:36). Her works were "good" (*agathos*) in the sense of being "truly beneficial."[3] Remember that "the good part," chosen by Mary of Bethany, was the beneficial Word of God.

Dorcas' good works included helping the poor. Luke uses a form of the Greek word eleos (mercy), which means she literally performed deeds of mercy. This term ranges in meaning from kind deeds to charitable giving. Dorcas may have been a wealthy woman who aided the poor financially, but we are told only that she made clothing for widows (Acts 9:39). We may assume Dorcas was a happy woman, for Jesus promised, "Blessed [happy] are the merciful" (Matthew 5:7). Lottie Beth Hobbs concurs: "Happy is the person who perceives his place in God's great scheme and fits into it with vigorous labor."[4]

Dorcas' service demonstrated authentic faith. To emphasize this, Luke added the phrase "which she did" (Acts 9:36). She didn't just *talk* about helping the poor. This servant-hearted woman would have removed the spider herself. She would have made the winter coat. Dorcas saw a need among the widows, and she sewed "tunics and garments" for them (v. 39). James describes such real faith:

> My brothers and sisters, if a person says that he has faith, but does nothing, then that faith is worth nothing. Can faith like that save him? No! A brother or sister in Christ might need clothes or might need food to eat. And you say to that person, "God be with you! I hope you stay warm and get plenty to eat." You say these things, but you don't give that person those things he needs. If you don't help that person, your words are worth nothing (James 2:14-16 ETRV).

Simply praying for the needy (without helping them) does not constitute service. Paul urged Christian women to be spiritually clothed "with good deeds, appropriate for women who profess to worship God" (1 Timothy 2:10 NIV). Dorcas was well dressed in her reputation as a doer of charitable deeds. Her profession of faith extended beyond the church walls. What a blessing she was to the Joppa congregation! Walton encourages imitation:

> A church without men and women who are willing to follow the example of Dorcas is an impoverished church. The creeds may be perfectly recited, the prayers eloquently prayed week after week … but these are not enough unless the church also has a few gazelles taking care of others, sending cards to shut-ins on their birthdays, baking communion bread for Sunday morning and knitting blankets for orphaned infants in Iraq.[5]

Is there a Dorcas in your congregation? Our congregation was blessed not only with Mabel but also with Annie Mae Johnson. She made quilts for Christian school benefits until her death in 2007 at the age of 106. Also there is Sylvia who, with her husband, gathers day-old baked goods from local grocers and distributes them to shut-ins. My great-aunt Rose did the same with vegetables in Yorba Linda, Calif., until her death at age 95. For two decades she fed a children's home. Christian service can be performed in creative ways.

What motivated Dorcas to serve? Herbert Lockyer suggests her good works flowed from a heart "grateful to God for His saving grace":

> [She] caught the vision of how she could serve Christ with her money and her needle. Dorcas knew what it was to have a regenerated heart and this was the source of her unselfish life and charitable acts. Behind her sewing of garments was a saved soul. Giving of alms, and the making of garments in themselves gain no merit with God, who, first of all, claims our hearts before our talents.[6]

Hearts full of thanksgiving find it easy to serve. Dorcas appreciated Christ's sacrifice, forgiveness of her sins, and hope of eternal salvation. She demonstrated her gratitude by doing what she could. She served the needy.

This explains why there was great mourning when Dorcas became sick and died (Acts 9:37, 39). Luke tells us nothing about her illness, but he mentions the timing: "[I]t happened in those days" (v. 37). R.C.H. Lenski proposes that "there was a divine providence in the fact that this death occurred at just this time. Peter was within reach."[7] Peter was about 10 miles away in Lydda and had just healed Aeneas, a man with palsy (vv. 32-35). Verse 38 states, "And since Lydda was near Joppa, and the disciples had heard that Peter was there, they sent two men to him, imploring him not to delay in coming to them."

Some suggest that the saints at Joppa only sought Peter's comfort and support in this time of sorrow.[8] But the urgency in their plea implies that they wanted a miracle. They washed Dorcas' body – with no mention of the usual anointing (John 19:40) – and "they laid her in an upper room" (Acts 9:37). Lenski comments on this departure from normal procedure:

We have no information to the effect that the bodies of the dead were usually placed in upper rooms before burial. Luke relates this in regard to Tabitha because an exception was made in her case. According to the regular custom she should have been buried soon after death; instead of that her body was kept until Peter could arrive. For this reason it was placed in the upper room.[9]

When Peter arrived, "they brought him to the upper room. And all the widows stood by him weeping, showing the tunics and garments which Dorcas had made while she was with them" (Acts 9:39). They may have been wearing the items. Widows of that day commonly belonged to the poorer class of society and were identified by special garments.[10] The tunics (*chitonas*) were garments worn closest to the body, and the garments (himatia, robes or cloaks) were worn over the other.[11] The widows in Joppa were paying tribute to Dorcas' memory. Lenski observes, "[H]ere, beside that loving heart and those busy hands that are now still in death, Peter is shown what this woman meant to the church and what the church had lost in her."[12] Dorcas was still very much needed.

Luke's words "which she did" (Acts 9:36), appearing in the durative imperfect tense, may emphasize that she "kept doing" these things. She served until she died. How many people retire from the Lord's work while they still live? Lockyer stresses that Dorcas died in the midst of a useful life – with her boots on, so to speak – and "with her needle in hand. What a way to go!"[13] The hymn "We'll Work Till Jesus Comes" reminds us that we must let our mortal body wear out (not rust out), knowing we will receive a new one in our heavenly home.

The Maturity-Building Discipline of Service

Service is very important in Christianity. Jesus taught this in word and deed. He said of Himself, "[T]he Son of man did not come to be served, but to serve" (Matthew 20:28). Serving others is not always easy or convenient. It involves action when a need arises.

As usual, Jesus met His disciples' needs on the night before His crucifixion. It was customary for hosts to wash guests' dirty feet. The way in which guests reclined at low U-shaped tables made clean feet a necessity. The disciples must have looked around the upper room wondering who would serve as the foot-washing "host." Jesus – the Son of God, who would serve them through death the very next day – picked up a basin of water and a towel and washed their feet. He encouraged them to follow His example:

> If I then, your Lord and Teacher, have washed your feet, you also ought to wash one another's feet. For I have given you an example, that you should do as I have done to you. Most assuredly, I say to you, a servant is not greater than his master; nor is he who is sent greater than he that sent him. If you know these things, blessed are you if you do them (John 13:14-17).

Through service we are blessed. Service produces spiritual maturity because it teaches humility and selflessness. Paul urged, "Be humble and give more honor to other people than to yourselves. Don't be interested only in your own life, but be interested in the lives of other people, too. In your lives you must think and act like Christ Jesus" (Philippians 2:3b-5 ETRV). We are most like Him when we serve.

Servant-hearted individuals do not demand their "rights." When Paul was shipwrecked on the island of Malta (Acts 28), he warmed himself by a fire built by someone else. As the blaze diminished, he didn't complain, "Somebody needs to bring some firewood!" No! He served. He got up and gathered sticks to keep the fire going. Consider the dying programs in your home congregation – the fires by which you have been warmed in years past. We must do our part to lay sticks on those fires. How else will future generations be warmed by them? Jesus washed feet. Paul gathered sticks. Dorcas made clothing. What can you do?

Dorcas practiced "[p]ure and undefiled religion" in her benevolent ministry (James 1:27). God has a special place in His heart for poor widows (Psalm 68:5). Scripture instructs relatives to care for their own widows, but the church must take care of those who have no financial support (1 Timothy 5:3-4). Paul urged Christians to "not let the church be burdened, that it may relieve those who are really widows" (v. 16). Is it right to wait for society to fill this need? W.M. Stratham, in *The Pulpit Commentary*, proposed that through the alms of the faithful, let the church counteract the neglect of the world.[14]

Dorcas was not guilty of neglect. She imitated Christ in compassionate service. Walton summarizes: "She took care of people. She made tunics and knitted afghans, baked cookies, held hands and visited people. She listened to the heartbreaks and joys, toils and triumphs of the people in the church at Joppa ... putting a human face on the compassion of Christ and expressing and embodying that love" for those in her village.[15] Today we are Jesus' arms and legs, reaching out and caring for the needs of others. Do our neighbors notice?

The people of Joppa noticed Dorcas. Lenski proposes that with her needle and thread she "fashioned a most important place for herself in the life of the young congregation."[16] They missed her. Simon J. Kistemaker observes that her death created a "void in the Christian community."[17] This was the perfect opportunity for a miracle to bring others to faith. Lenski agrees, "The Lord intended to distinguish this humble woman in a signal way, namely by raising her from the dead. He had given much to the church in Joppa when he gave her to it; now he intended to give the church still more in her."[18]

Benefits of Dorcas' Service: A Resurrected Servant and a Town Led to Christ

Do you know women whose distinctive fragrance lingers after they leave a room? Lockyer has made such a comparison to Dorcas' memory: "The vessel containing the costly ointment was broken, and the odor filled the house as never before."[19] Proverbs 31:31 states that the works of the virtuous woman "praise her in the gates," and Revelation 14:13 assures us that our good works follow us into heaven. Dorcas was on her way to her heavenly reward, but God had a different plan.

Peter sent everyone out of the room where Dorcas' body lay. The disciples had been given the power to perform miracles, and he asked God for a resurrection. Compare the scene with Jesus' healing of Jairus' daughter in Mark 5:

> But Peter put them all out, and knelt down and prayed. And turning to the body he said, "Tabitha, arise." And she opened her eyes, and when she saw Peter she sat up (Acts 9:40).

> But when He had put them all outside, He took the father and the mother of the child, and those who were with Him, and entered where the child was lying. Then He took the child by the hand, and said to her, "Talitha cumi," which is translated, "Little girl, I say to you, arise." Immediately the girl arose (Mark 5:40-42).

Jesus let the child's parents stay in the room. Peter sent everyone out. Jesus, who touched even lepers, took the hand of Jairus' daughter. Peter did not touch Dorcas, for a Jew was considered unclean if he touched the dead (Haggai 2:13). Jesus healed the little girl. Peter humbly asked God to work through him.[20] Lenski asserts,

> In every case the Lord and his Spirit directed those to whom the gift of performing miracles had been granted, and they proceeded only when and where they were so directed. What the Lord's will was in the case of Tabitha none presumed to say, and we shall see that Peter himself did not at first know. So in all that prompted the message to Peter their thought was only to bow to the Lord's will while trusting in his boundless grace.[21]

Peter spoke two words to Dorcas: "Tabitha, arise." Similarly, Jesus said, "Little girl, I say to you, arise." In both cases, the dead arose. Peter gave Dorcas his hand "and lifted her up; and when he had called the saints and widows, he presented her alive" (Acts 9:41).

Imagine the rejoicing! Who could keep this good news to herself? Acts 9:42 says, "And it became known throughout all Joppa, and many believed on the Lord." If anyone had not known about Dorcas' good works, he or she certainly knew now – and learned about her God. It is rightly asserted that Christian service is "the way the world discovers the love of God."[22] The story is told about a World War II soldier walking through a bombed European city. He found a starving child and gave the boy some of his rations. The boy looked up at him and asked, "Sir, are you God?" The people of Joppa learned about God's love and power through this incident.

Dorcas touched many lives. She was just an ordinary woman, quietly going about her service to the Lord. But the impact she made was monumental. "Dorcas was not a preacher, theologian or eloquent writer. She did not make her mark on the church with brave deeds or financial gifts," writes Walton. "But she did win converts and touch lives and probably influenced more people than anyone else in Joppa."[23] If a person wants to make a difference in this world, all she needs is a servant heart. Martin Luther King Jr. concurred: "[E]verybody can be great because everybody can serve. You don't have to have a college degree to serve. ... You don't have to make your subject and verb agree to serve. ... You only need a heart full of grace, a soul generated by love."[24]

Dorcas found her niche in the kingdom. She took Jesus' message personally when He said, "I was naked and you clothed Me" (Matthew 25:36). Lockyer describes Dorcas as a servant "who with her needle embroidered her name ineffaceably into the beneficence of the world."[25]

The world still takes note. The Dorcas Society, a worldwide ministry named in her honor, provides clothing to the poor. The original organization was founded Dec. 1, 1834, in Douglas, Isle of Man, as a public thanksgiving to God for the "merciful exemption" of the town from a cholera outbreak at the time.[26] The group replaced clothing and bedding of the poor that had been burned in order to stop the spread of disease in the community. Lockyer concludes that the organization's namesake, Dorcas, the saintly benefactress, was "unconscious of the magnificent work she was doing and of its far-reaching consequences. Dorcas did not aspire to be a leader but was content to stay in her own home and try to do all she could in all the ways she could."[27]

What can you do? Sew for the poor? Contribute financially to help them? Provide food? Anyone can serve, and everyone should. It is a humbling, maturity-building exercise. Are you willing to wash feet? Are you willing to remove a spider? Are you willing to serve when there is a need? May God help us to participate in true biblical service.

Reflection Questions

1. Discuss Dorcas' influence in Joppa before and after her death.

2. List other servant-hearted people in Scripture and the works they performed.

3. Name some "dirty jobs" or "thankless duties" in your church and community in which volunteers serve.

4. List dying or struggling programs in your congregation in need of someone to lay sticks on the fire.

5. What God-given talent(s) do you possess? How might you use them in serving others?

Spiritual Exercise

Participate in a service project for a widow in your family or congregation. Consider these suggestions adapted from June Wesley in her *20th Century Christian* article "A Lonely Widow."[28]

1. Bring food when she is sick.

2. Send flowers for her birthday, Christmas or New Year's Day.

3. Send notes of encouragement.

4. Take her with you when you shop or run other errands.

5. Pray with her at home or over the phone.

6. Talk with her on the phone – or just listen.

7. Send magazine subscriptions.

8. Take her to lunch, or for coffee or dessert.

9. Give or loan her books, tapes or CDs.

10. Take her to the doctor.

11. Help with upkeep around her house.

12. Help her with hospital bills.

Chapter 6

Rewarding Hospitality
Rahab

Joshua 2:1-24; James 2:25

S ome women are just naturally hospitable. Vearl and Armina come to mind in our congregation. Almost every member has enjoyed a delicious meal at the table of this mother and daughter. Who in your congregation may be linked to the idea of Christian hospitality?

From Scripture you might think of Mary and Martha meeting Jesus' needs or the widow who made a room for Elisha. But what about Rahab the prostitute? Would she be on your list? She took in two Israelite spies when they needed protection. Why? Was it simply to save her life during the siege of Jericho? Or did she recognize the sovereignty of Israel's God and welcome an opportunity to serve Him? Let's examine her story.

The Scriptures' Message

The biblical record begins: "Now Joshua the son of Nun sent out two men from Acacia Grove to spy secretly, saying, 'Go, view the land, especially Jericho.' So they went, and came to the house of a harlot named Rahab, and lodged there" (Joshua 2:1). The Lord promised to give Israel the land of the Canaanites

(Exodus 13:11). Because Jericho was the first city to conquer, Joshua sent the spies.

Like other ancient cities, Jericho had places where strangers could find food and lodging. Rahab's house must have been such a place, which most likely served the additional purpose of sexual accommodation. The author described Rahab as a harlot. Unlike Israelite women, this pagan lived in disobedience to God's Law. David Merling asserts that Rahab was even "an outcast in Jericho":

> The title "prostitute" contrasts Rahab, as a low-living non-Israelite, with Israelite women, who were commanded not to be prostitutes (Leviticus 19:29; Deuteronomy 23:18). Her profession also highlights her as part of the lower strata of society. Even in Mesopotamian society, which considered sexual license to be the natural, expected condition, prostitutes were placed on the same social level as sorcerers, lunatics, eccentrics and demoniacs.[1]

The text does not imply that the two spies engaged in illicit activity with Rahab. Elie Assis suggests that it simply says they " 'lay [down] there' instead of the similar, but more sexual 'lay with her.' "[2] Perhaps God led them to Rahab's house. He knew the heart of its owner.

The two strangers drew some attention in Jericho. That very night, reports came to the king, "Behold, men have come here tonight from the children of Israel to search out the country" (Joshua 2:2). The Canaanites were afraid because they had heard about Israel's powerful God. Verse 11 reveals that their hearts melted; "neither did there remain any more courage in anyone" because of them. Jericho's worried king immediately sent messengers to Rahab's house (v. 3). However, when they arrived, she hid the spies under stalks of flax on her rooftop (v. 6). Flax was a plant in Palestine used to manufacture linen and as food for cattle. Having piles of it on the rooftop of an inn would not be unusual.

The king's men demanded of Rahab, "Bring out the men who

have come to you, who have entered your house, for they have come to search out all the country" (Joshua 2:3). The "quicker-witted prostitute"[3] answered, "Yes, the men came to me, but I did not know where they were from. And it happened as the gate was being shut, when it was dark, that the men went out. Where the men went I do not know; pursue them quickly, for you may overtake them" (vv. 4-5).

Some suggest that when Rahab told the king's messengers the "men came to me" (Joshua 2:4), she was leading them to assume they came, received sexual favors and left. Assis writes:

> By means of this lie Rahab rejects any suspicion that she has cooperated with the spies, suggesting rather that they came, like most of her visitors, for sexual satisfaction, and, when their desires were met, they left. If she had not lied, but rather claimed that there had been no sexual intercourse, and that the spies had come to lodge at the inn, she could not claim that they had already left. The apparent sexual intentions of the spies constitute a good alibi for Rahab's claim that she did not know where they came from (Joshua 2:4).[4]

Rahab's deception worked. The king's men left. Scripture reveals that they headed toward Jordan, to the fords, to look for the spies, and the gate was shut behind them (v. 7).

Rahab performed a service for Israel by protecting the spies from interrogation. Before the men lay down to sleep, she explained why she helped them. Some have called her monologue "Rahab's Acclamation" (Joshua 2:9-13).[5] She declared, "I know that the LORD has given you the land, that the terror of you has fallen on us" (v. 9). Then she explained what she and all the inhabitants of the land had heard about Him:

> For we have heard how the LORD dried up the water of the Red Sea for you when you came out of Egypt, and what you did to the two kings of the Amorites who were on the other side of the Jordan, Sihon and Og, whom you utterly destroyed. And as soon as we

heard these things, our hearts melted; neither did there remain any more courage in anyone because of you, for the LORD your God, He is God in heaven above and on earth beneath (Joshua 2:10-11).

Perhaps Israel's victory hymn, titled "The Song of Moses" (Exodus 15:1-19), had been heard throughout Canaan. Rahab's words are strikingly similar to those of Moses in verses 14-18:

> The people will hear and be afraid; Sorrow will take hold of the inhabitants of Philistia. Then the chiefs of Edom will be dismayed; The mighty men of Moab, Trembling will take hold of them; All the inhabitants of Canaan will melt away. Fear and dread will fall on them; By the greatness of Your arm They will be as still as a stone, Till Your people pass over, O LORD, Till the people pass over Whom You have purchased. You will bring them in and plant them In the mountain of Your inheritance, In the place, O LORD, which You have made For Your own dwelling, The sanctuary, O Lord, which Your hands have established. The LORD shall reign forever and ever.

Rahab made a great confession: "[T]he LORD your God, He is God in heaven above and on earth beneath" (Joshua 2:11). If she had idols, she gave them up, for in this acclamation she acknowledged Jehovah as God. Rabbinic tradition teaches that her generosity to the spies demonstrated her "repentance and conversion to Israel's God."[6]

The second part of "Rahab's Acclamation" suggests another motivation for protecting the spies: survival. Knowing that even Jericho's mighty wall was no match for Israel's God, she begged,

> Now therefore, I beg you, swear to me by the LORD since I have shown you kindness, that you also will show kindness to my father's house, and give me a true token, and spare my father, my mother, my brothers, my sisters, and all that they have, and deliver our lives from death (Joshua 2:12-13).

This is a testimony to Rahab's faith not only in God's power but in His mercy. For this she was rewarded.

The two spies told Rahab that God would protect her and her family during the seige of Jericho. They promised "[o]ur lives for yours" (Joshua 2:14) if she met three conditions: (1) She must mark her house with a scarlet cord; (2) she must stay indoors with her family on that day; and (3) she must keep their visit a secret (vv. 18-20). Rahab agreed to follow their instructions. The spies then followed her advice to hide three days in the mountain until the king's soldiers stopped looking for them (v. 22).

In Joshua 6 we read that Israel marched around Jericho seven days. Verses 16-17 reveal what happened on the final day:

> And the seventh time it happened, when the priests blew the trumpets, that Joshua said to the people: "Shout, for the LORD has given you the city! Now the city shall be doomed by the LORD to destruction, it and all who are in it. Only Rahab the harlot shall live, she and all who are with her in the house, because she hid the messengers that we sent."

Israel shouted, and God caused the walls of Jericho to fall down. His people walked over the flattened walls. They killed every man and woman in Jericho, except those in the house with the scarlet thread in the window – the house of Rahab. Scripture points out that Rahab was personally delivered by the two spies:

> But Joshua had said to the two men who had spied out the country, "Go into the harlot's house, and from there bring out the woman and all that she has, as you swore to her." And the young men who had been spies went in and brought out Rahab, her father, her mother, her brothers, and all that she had. So they brought out all her relatives and left them outside the camp of Israel (Joshua 6:22-23).

Afterward, Israel burned Jericho to the ground. Archaeology confirms the biblical account that the wall "fell beneath itself" (Joshua 6:20). The website www.answersingenesis.org reports the findings of British archaeologist Kathleen Kenyon (1950s), who revealed "there is ample evidence that the mudbrick city wall collapsed and was deposited at the base of the stone retaining wall at the time the city met its end."[7] The website also explains how Rahab's house (located on or against the wall) was spared: "The German excavation of 1907–1909 found that on the north a short stretch of the lower city wall did not fall as everywhere else. A portion of that mudbrick wall was still standing to a height of over two meters (eight feet)." Kenyon also reported evidence that the city was burned afterward:

> The destruction was complete. Walls and floors were blackened or reddened by fire, and every room was filled with fallen bricks, timbers, and household utensils; in most rooms the fallen debris was heavily burnt, but the collapse of the walls of the eastern rooms seems to have taken place before they were affected by the fire."[8]

Here is an interesting sidenote. Joshua 6:26 says Joshua placed a curse on anyone who tried to rebuild the city. It states that whoever did would "lay its foundation with his firstborn, and with his youngest he shall set up its gates." This meant the foundation and gates would be rebuilt at the cost of life.[9] First Kings 16:34 presents a fulfillment of that prophecy: "In his days Hiel of Bethel built Jericho. He laid its foundation with Abiram his firstborn, and with his youngest son Segub he set up its gates, according to the word of the LORD, which He had spoken through Joshua the son of Nun." Promises made by God's people in Scripture were always kept. This truth applied to the spies' promise to Rahab. Hebrews 11:31 confirms, "By faith the harlot Rahab did not perish with those who did not believe, when she had received the spies with peace."

The Maturity-Building
Discipline of Hospitality

Just as God approved of Rahab for her service to the Israelite spies, He desires such willingness from Christians today: "Be hospitable to one another without grumbling" (1 Peter 4:9). The reason some complain about hospitality is that having people in one's home is not convenient. Ajith Fernando, in *The NIV Application Commentary*, explains the objection by guests:

> The most frequently heard objection to staying in homes of Christians when traveling is how tiring it can be to spend time talking with the hosts. I think we used to call this fellowship! But today we strictly regulate fellowship so that we can control it according to our well-planned schedules. Long conversations with our hosts are one of the best ways to identify with the people to whom we are ministering.[10]

When arriving the night before ladies day engagements, I enjoy staying in members' homes rather than hotels. Not only is it safer for a woman traveling alone, but it has provided some of the most wonderful experiences of my life. Heaven will be sweeter when bonds of friendship are renewed in eternity with the women who have demonstrated their hospitality to me.

Christian hospitality also includes sharing meals with others in our homes. My mother always invited the visiting gospel preacher for her delicious fried chicken dinner, and I was greatly influenced by these biblical scholars sitting at our table. Sadly, this is becoming a lost art. Eugene Peterson writes, "The practice of hospitality has fallen on bad times. Fewer and fewer families sit down to a meal together. The meal, which used to be a gathering place for families, neighbors and 'the stranger at the gate,' is on its way out."[11]

Have we become guilty of Martha's worry and trouble with much serving? It has been said that we get so stressed with cleaning, shopping, and creating the perfect table setting that it's no wonder the word "hospital" is found in "hospitality." Let us realize that restaurants and hotels are no substitute for one's responsibility to be hospitable.

Has shallow talk with our spiritual brothers and sisters and neighbors replaced the closeness that comes with eating together? There is an adage, "You never know a person until you have your feet under his table." Laurel Sewell, in *The Six Gifts of Hospitality*, reminds us that sitting around a table can nourish our spirits as well as our bodies.[12] Her book includes a thought-provoking quote by Jan des Bouvrie of Opsij, Netherlands:

> My philosophy is that true intimacy and romance always flourish at tables, not on sofas. At the table you have the best eye contact, and that's what it's all about. People push their empty plates to one side and linger longer and longer at the table. Once, people used to move from the dining room to the couch. That was a disaster because all the intimacy they had built up disappeared and they had to start all over. A table is the most beautiful piece of furniture there is.[13]

Laurel remembers dinners at her grandparents' home when the women would sit together and eat. She writes, "This provided a relaxed time for talk among the women. … I sometimes wish for that unhurried time of sharing among the women about things that were common among them, and the passing of traditions from one generation to the next."[14] Consider the benefits of female companionship in our cozy kitchens, where we can refill our dessert plates and linger as long as we want.

Let us not forget Peter's second phrase in 1 Peter 4:9: "without grumbling." Benjamin Franklin wrote in *Poor Richard's Almanack*, "If you wou'd have Guests merry with your cheer, Be so your self, or so at least appear."[15] Serving guests should not be burdensome. Sewell reminds us, "Real hospitality is not dependent on silver service or matching towels, but on kindness, warm hearts and a desire to meet the needs of others."[16] Perhaps changing our perspective would help. Hospitality is a good work that reaps three benefits:

(1) *Through hospitality, we refresh others.* Our world is

becoming very impersonal. Loneliness is widespread. Depression is epidemic. Since drive-thru and online shopping began, people rarely walk into shops and chat leisurely as our grandmothers did. Many people are starving for personal contact and relationship. Hospitality creates great opportunities to "reach out and touch someone" for Christ. Paul was thankful for those who had refreshed him in his discouraging ministry (1 Corinthians 16:18; 2 Timothy 1:16).

(2) *Through hospitality, we build relationships.* One sure way to have guests is simply to invite them. Then we must prepare. If you've had your house listed for sale, you understand the self-discipline required to show it at a moment's notice. In congregations with whom we've worked, my husband and I invited members into our home for monthly "birthday fellowships." All those with birthdays (and their families) were invited for cake. Our children have special memories of these fellowships in our Myrtle Beach, S.C., ministry, especially December 1992. The Air Force Base still existed, and one of our members was to be deployed in Desert Storm. With his cake, we served a big steak. He really felt special! That's what hospitality is all about.

(3) *Through hospitality, we ourselves are refreshed.* Anytime we do good, it comes back to us: "[W]ith the measure you use, it will be measured back to you" (Matthew 7:2). Luke 14:13 tells us to invite the poor, maimed, lame and blind. God will repay. Sometimes we need refreshment ourselves that comes from intimate fellowship. When my husband Steven and I were newlyweds, I dutifully invited the widowed, new converts and visitors to our home; but – living in California, miles away from my family in North Carolina – I needed encouragement, too. We began inviting young couples and godly mentors as well. As a result, we were refreshed and established friendships that have withstood time and distance.

I hope these three benefits of hospitality will inspire readers. Remember, the idea is not to impress but to serve. This was what Rahab did. And she was rewarded by the Lord.

Benefits of Rahab's Hospitality:
Salvation and Inclusion in Christ's Ancestry

Rahab was a sinful, pagan prostitute. She might have said with Paul that among sinners, "I am chief" (1 Timothy 1:15). Yet when she learned about Jehovah, she confessed His name and demonstrated her faith through action. She helped the Israelite spies escape from her window by a scarlet cord (Joshua 2:15, 18). Liz Curtis Higgs, in her article "Rahab: A Hooker With a Heart for God," points out the significance of the cord color: "Scarlet. Now there's a color that makes a statement. 'Though your sins are like scarlet … ' (Isaiah 1:18). Rahab's sins were scarlet, all right, yet washed clean by the God she trusted to save her and all whom she loved." [17]

God showed approval of Rahab. He placed her name among the list of faithful Old Testament men and women in Hebrews 11:31. He forgave her of her harlotry and of her lie to the king's messengers. For some this latter sin remains a blemish on her good work. John MacArthur, in his book *Twelve Extraordinary Women*, suggests that it "morally tainted" her act of harboring the spies.[18] Others justify Rahab's lie. Allen Verhey, in his article "Is Lying Always Wrong?" suggests that her activity in hiding the spies equated to making a covenant with them:

> She covenanted to hide the Israelites from the tyrant who threatened to harm them. That same tyrant put her in a position of having either to break that covenant or to tell a lie. The tyrant was at fault here, putting her in a situation of either violating covenant or telling a lie – and her lie, another kind of violence, may be permitted as a form of covenanted self-defense.[19]

Scripture does not condone Rahab's lie. It simply shows the imperfections of its heroes and heroines. Abraham and Sarah lied (Genesis 12:13; 20:2; 18:15), and they are listed among God's most faithful (Hebrews 11:8, 11). Abraham was justified by his obedient works (Romans 4:2; James 2:21). So was Rahab. C.F. Keil explains that "a lie is always a sin" and, therefore, no matter what the reason, "the course which she adopted was a sin of weakness, which was forgiven her in mercy because of her faith.[20] James 2:25 confirms: "Likewise, was not Rahab the harlot also justified by works when she received the messengers and sent them out another way?"

God honored the Israelite spies' promise to deliver Rahab. He knew her heart. Joshua 6:25 summarizes: "And Joshua spared Rahab the harlot, her father's household, and all that she had. So she dwells in Israel to this day, because she hid the messengers whom Joshua sent to spy out Jericho." The phrase "to this day" is significant, for Rahab had joined herself to God's covenant people and was still there when Joshua wrote this biblical account (24:26). K.M. Campbell observes that by means of Rahab's covenant in Joshua 2, she and her family became members of the Israelite covenant community forever.[21]

The "harlot turned heroine" became an integral part of Israel's history. David Merling proposes that her "role in the Jericho story is one of the most significant events in which all Israel participated."[22] Not only was Rahab blessed to be part of God's people, but she was also included in the ancestral lineage of Jesus Christ. Read Matthew 1:1-6 to find Jesus' genealogy from Abraham to Salmon, the Israelite who married Rahab. Verse 5 reveals that Rahab became the mother of Boaz (who married Ruth), grandmother of Obed, great-grandmother of Jesse, and great-great-grandmother of King David.[23] God accepts the obedient into His kingdom, no matter what their past.

He also blesses those who show hospitality. Some, like Vearl and Armina, are just naturally hospitable. Others, like Rahab, may be providentially "commandeered" into such service.[24] Did she serve simply to save her own neck during the siege of Jericho? Or did she recognize the sovereignty of Israel's God and welcome this opportunity to serve? Maybe both. But through her hospitality, she still serves as a biblical role model for us today.

Reflection Questions

1. Discuss Rahab's motivation to hide the spies.

2. How difficult do you think it was for Rahab to tell no one in Jericho that her household would be saved during the siege? Contrast her with Noah's wife.

3. Do you believe hospitality is a lost art? Explain.

4. Discuss the benefits of inviting people into homes instead of eating at restaurants and staying in hotels.

5. Discuss Rahab's assimilation into Israelite society. Compare this to that of new converts.

Spiritual Exercise

Practice hospitality. Invite a group of widows or widowers into your home for hot vegetable soup in winter or chicken salad and croissants with fruit in summer. Let each of them share with the group something interesting about themselves.

Chapter 7

Difficult Waiting
Sarah

Genesis 16; 18:1-15; 21:1-7; Hebrews 11:11

Waiting can be difficult – especially when prayer petitions are involved. When I was young, my sisters and I prayed for Daddy to become a Christian. I waited for an answer. During my 20s, living miles away and busy with ministry and children, I continued to pray for Daddy. I waited and waited. However, during my early 30s my faith wavered, and I gave up. Then, one Sunday my husband preached a sermon about a father asking Jesus to heal his son (Mark 9:14-29). Jesus told him, "If you can believe, all things are possible to him who believes" (v. 23). The father replied, "Lord, I believe; help my unbelief (*apistia*, "lack of faith")!" (v. 24). He recognized that his faith was weak and in need of strengthening. Jesus answered his prayer. His son was healed! After listening to that sermon, I renewed my prayer for Daddy, asking, "Father, I believe; but I need a stronger faith." Soon things began to happen to change Daddy's heart.

Faith is necessary for answered prayer. James 1:6-7 tells us, "But let him ask in faith, with no doubting, for he who doubts is like a wave of the sea driven and tossed by the wind. For let not that man suppose that he will receive anything from the Lord." Sometimes faith must be demonstrated in the exercise of waiting. This is easier said than done. We need God's help – and He does help. Psalm 27:14 urges, "Wait on the LORD; Be of good courage, and He shall strengthen your heart; Wait, I say, on the LORD!"

One particular woman in Scripture learned this lesson the hard way. She found waiting on the Lord difficult and decided to help Him fulfill His promise. However, her actions resulted in one of the most disastrous consequences in history.

Her birth name was Sarai, but God changed it to Sarah (Genesis 17:15). She was a unique Old Testament character, chosen by God to become "the joint fountainhead of the great Jewish race."[1] From this woman a special multitude would spring.

Sarah was a woman of physical and spiritual beauty, desired by kings and commended as an example of reverent submission for Christian women (Genesis 12:14-15; 20:2; 1 Peter 3:6). Although Abraham was not perfect, Sarah honored his position as husband. With him, she left their home to spend the rest of her life in a foreign land (Genesis 12:4-5). Lottie Beth Hobbs explains, "Together with her husband, Sarah accepted this unprecedented challenge to take a new step of faith and follow God into the unknown. She also had to leave friends and loved ones and familiar surroundings to face the perils and anxieties of an uncertain future."[2] In Hebrews 11:11, Sarah is listed among the Old Testament faithful.

However, Scripture reveals that Sarah was not always full of faith. Donald Guthrie observes, "It is perhaps surprising to find Sarah spoken of as an example of faith, for according to Genesis she was more conspicuous as an example of doubt."[3] The Genesis account helps us understand why the Bible speaks about her faith.

The Scriptures' Message

When God promised Abraham, "I will make you a great nation" and "[t]o your descendants I will give this land," Sarah must have been elated (Genesis 12:2, 7). She was 65 years old and barren (11:30; 12:4; 17:17). Can't you imagine her knitting little blue booties while she waited to conceive? She waited and waited. After about 10 years, her faith wavered and she gave up (12:4; 16:16). Herbert Lockyer comments on her sad plight: "[T]he possibility of ever becoming a mother died in her heart."[4]

Perhaps, realizing that her name was not mentioned in the covenant promise, Sarah thought God did not intend her to bear Abraham's child. Eugenia Price surmises, "I'm sure Sarai wanted to believe it, but to her practical mind, the facts were all against it: she was just too old. And so, she figured, before Abram was too old also they had better do the practical thing and help God along."[5] Therefore, Sarah devised a scheme to fulfill the promise by "renting the womb" of another.[6] She told Abraham: "See now, the LORD has restrained me from bearing children. Please, go in to my maid; perhaps I shall obtain children by her" (Genesis 16:2). Sarah's plan fit with common ancient attitudes about conception.

First, she believed that the Lord had closed her womb. God did open and close wombs in certain cases (Genesis 20:18; 29:31; 30:22; 1 Samuel 1:5), and the ancient world attributed all blessings and curses directly to Him (Job 4:7-9). This should not discourage women today. John H. Walton points out that medical causes connected to a fallen world can work against this blessing, and "[t]herefore, an infertile woman should not be considered (by herself or others) to be under God's judgment."[7] God had His reasons for letting Sarah wait.

Second, surrogacy was common in ancient Mesopotamian culture (Ur and Haran). Their laws specified, "[I]f a man's wife could not have a child of her own, she could commit her slave girl to her husband; he could have sexual relations with her, and any child born to that relationship would be regarded as the wife's legal child."[8] In old Assyrian and Nuzi marriage contracts, this was not only appropriate but "contractually dictated" if a wife was barren.[9] The ancient world had the misunderstanding that a man deposited the "seed" (early embryo) into a woman, and she served as an "incubator" for the baby.[10] Because one incubator worked as well as another, people considered this kind of surrogacy a legitimate option.[11] So did Sarah. She urged Abraham to lie with her handmaid.

Third, Sarah supposed that through Hagar, her own dynasty might be "built up." John T. Willis has explained this Old Testament legal concept:

> The law in Deuteronomy 25:5-10 states that if brothers live together and one brother dies, the dead man's brother must marry his widow (v. 5), bear children by her (v. 6), and thus perpetuate his brother's name in Israel (vv. 6-7, the Levirate law). But if the living brother refuses to marry his dead brother's widow, she shall go up to him in the presence of the elders, take his sandal off, spit in his face, and say, "So shall it be done to the man who does not build up [*yibhneh*] his brother's house" (vv. 8-9). Here, to "build up" a brother's house (v. 9) means the same thing as to "bear" a son or children by his brother's wife (v. 6). Logically, then, to "to be built up" by one's handmaid means for the handmaid to bear children to one's husband.[12]

Fourth, Sarah did not realize her lack of faith. She may have believed her duty was to fulfill her childbearing in this way. She was a good woman whom Scripture holds up as a model of love and respect for her husband (1 Peter 3:6). Katherine L. Cook suggests that perhaps love moved Sarah to offer Hagar:

> With what had to be an act of selflessness, she decided that the only way Abraham could become a father was through another woman. … She must have loved Abraham a great deal to make such a sacrifice. She must have known how important Abraham's God was to him and how he looked for the fulfillment of God's covenantal promise. We who know the end of the story can easily declare her to be foolish and even callous, but how many of us would wait until it seemed impossible for our prayers to be answered without taking action ourselves?[13]

Thomas Whitelaw, in *The Pulpit Commentary*, concurs, suggesting that for Sarah the practice was common, the motive was good, and the self-denial was great.[14]

However, the truth is that Sarah doubted God. Lockyer agrees: "The attempt to secure the Child of Promise by Hagar was the result of a lack of faith in God's omnipotence."[15] Abraham must have doubted, too, for he followed through with Sarah's plan. Hagar bore him a son named Ishmael (Genesis 16:15). This event, caused by Sarah's failure to wait, produced a result similar to Eve's transgression in the Garden of Eden. Both actions produced unhappy family life, and both negatively impacted the world. George Van Pelt Campbell, in his article "Rushing Ahead of God," writes, "Human schemes that depart from God's ways often backfire and produce bitterness and suffering."[16]

Bitterness aptly describes the relationship that developed between Sarah and Hagar. (This tension will be discussed more fully in Chapter 8.) But it appears that Sarah's faithless action had a more lasting effect. Scholars suggest it prompted a hatred that continues today between the descendants of Hagar's son, Ishmael, and Sarah's future son, Isaac. Guy N. Woods has described it this way:

> Abraham, through Hagar, in the birth of Ishmael, became the father of the Arab peoples. Abraham, through Sarah, in the birth of Isaac, became the father of the Jewish peoples. Their mothers hated each other; their children have hated, despised and often fought each other ever since. In this manner and with these results did the troubles between the Arabs and the Jews, now so sorely plaguing the Middle East, begin with Sarah's efforts to extricate God from what she supposed to be an insoluble difficulty![17]

Sarah's example shows that a foolish attempt to obtain blessing her way "results in the Ishmael, not the Isaac."[18] If Sarah had simply been patient – if she had not pushed God's timetable – she could have avoided much heartache and enjoyed the blessed hope, joy and satisfaction that come from waiting on the Lord.

The Maturity-Building Discipline of Waiting

Have you ever waited for an answer to a special prayer petition? Scripture tells us, "Wait on the LORD" (Psalm 27:14). But, according to Neale Pryor, "Often the greatest test of our faith is waiting. The silence of God is sometimes the hardest part of life to deal with. It is hard to realize that God does not run on the same schedule that humans do."[19]

In 1989, Rosemary McKnight wrote an insightful book titled *Those Who Wait*. Its writing was prompted by a difficult waiting period in her life. In the book she discusses disappointment, discouragement and questions that naturally arise: "Why has this happened to us?" "What is the purpose in this?" "Where is God leading us?" and "When will our waiting be over?"[20] One particular verse gave her strength: "But those who wait on the LORD Shall renew their strength; They shall mount up with wings like eagles, They shall run and not be weary, They shall walk and not faint" (Isaiah 40:31). Rosemary assures us that our waiting has a purpose. Her story had a happy ending, for as she and her husband patiently resided in "God's waiting room," they found it to be a time of preparation and growth.[21] They took advantage of educational opportunities that led to exciting life changes!

Scripture includes accounts of others who waited on the Lord. Joseph is my favorite. When sold by his brothers into slavery, he prayed and waited on the Lord for rescue. During his imprisonment after Potiphar's wife falsely accused him, he again prayed and waited on the Lord. His waiting period was God's plan to put him in the right place at the right time for a special work. Moses is another example. God placed him in a 40-year waiting room, baby-sitting sheep in the desert until he was ready to baby-sit an immature multitude of God's people in the same desert. Our waiting has a purpose. Are you struggling in God's waiting room? Wait on the Lord. It is an exercise that teaches patience (James 1:2-4).

Sarah is a model of what not to do. She did not wait on the Lord, and she regretted it. She found out, as Irene Taylor points out, that "[i]t is always a mistake to try to rush God's timetable.

It is always a mistake to try to change God's plan."[22] But her scheme did not stop God from fulfilling His promise. Lockyer cleverly observes, "[A]ll poor Hagar could do was produce an Ishmael. It was only through Sarah that the promised seed could come."[23] God would bless Sarah with the child of promise when He was ready.

Benefits of Sarah's Waiting: Motherhood and the Promised Seed

Good things come to those who wait. Because Sarah assumed that God's promise was fulfilled through Ishmael, she waited for Abraham's blessings to come through him. During nearly 15 years of family tension, she waited (Genesis 16:16; 17:17). Then God – who keeps His promises – reaffirmed His covenant with Abraham (17:1-21). The son of promise was about to be conceived. Verse 17 states, "Then Abraham fell on his face and laughed, and said in his heart, 'Shall a child be born to a man who is one hundred years old? And shall Sarah, who is ninety years old, bear a child?" Did you know that Abraham laughed? Yes, he also had doubts, but in God's time Sarah would bear this son.

Read Genesis 17:15-21. Note the specific inclusion of Sarah's name in the covenant promise. On this occasion God changed their names from Abram to Abraham and from Sarai ("my princess") to Sarah ("princess") (vv. 5, 15). Whitelaw explains, "[W]hereas formerly she was Abram's princess only, she was henceforth to be recognized as a princess generally."[24] Such personal identification changes made by God are called "sacramental names." Lockyer defined these as "names given by God Himself, or under His inspiration in association with a particular promise, covenant or declaration of His, as to the character, destiny or mission of those distinctly named. Thus, a sacramental name became a sign and seal of an established covenant between God and the recipient of such a name."[25] Obviously, Abraham told Sarah about his conversation with God, the name changes, and the covenant reaffirmation. But she still doubted. She needed a faith lift. A visit from the Lord Himself was required "to establish Sarah's faith in the promise that she should bear a son in her old age."[26]

Genesis 18 records the incident in Mamre. Three guests visited Abraham's tent (v. 2). As they ate under a tree, they asked, "Where is Sarah your wife?" (vv. 8-9). Of course, the all-knowing guest knew that Sarah was behind the tent door listening to their conversation. Perhaps He wanted to get her attention, for His next statement would specifically involve her. Or maybe He wanted His hosts to realize that He was the omniscient Lord. A stranger would not have known the name of Abraham's wife.

Sarah heard the Lord's announcement: "I will come again in the spring. At that time, your wife Sarah will have a son" (Genesis 18:10 ETRV). Still doubting, Sarah laughed to herself. This was a likely reaction, for she was old and past the age of childbearing (v. 11). Bruce K. Waltke describes her body as "procreatively dead."[27] Her response is paraphrased, "Can an old, 'withered' woman still bear children?"[28]

Sarah doubted. The Lord, who knew her thoughts, personally addressed her lack of faith: "Why did Sarah laugh? … Is anything too hard for the LORD?" (Genesis 18:13-14). We have compared this phrase to the one Gabriel proclaimed centuries later while informing Mary about Elizabeth's pregnancy: "For with God nothing will be impossible" (Luke 1:37).

Sarah was shocked at the Lord's rebuke. She replied, "I did not laugh." And He responded, "No, but you did laugh!" (Genesis 18:15). Sarah not only doubted; she lied. As we learned in Rahab's account, Scripture does not cover up the sins of biblical heroines. Bobbie Jobe comments, "Sarah was a woman of the flesh just like you, with both weaknesses and strengths. One of the beautiful things about the Bible is that we are told both the good points and bad points about each character."[29] Perhaps Sarah is a spiritual role model precisely because she was imperfect yet willing to trust. Charles L. Brown proposes that she "left an example by rising above her sins and failures in life."[30] No matter what we have done in life, God can forgive us of our sins and accept our service in His kingdom.

Sarah did not answer the Lord's rebuke. Her silence, according to Richard Spencer, "was an evidence of her conviction; her subsequent conception was a proof of her repentance and forgiveness." [31] She was suddenly struck with the realization that the Lord who could read her thoughts could also open her womb. [32] He was affirming that she would bear the child of promise within a year. Her faith was strengthened.

Sarah's transformed faith moved her to action. As we learned in the lesson about Dorcas, "faith without works is dead" (James 2:20). John H. Tietjen suggests that Sarah's trust "expressed itself in action, in the intimacy of the marriage bed." [33] We know her faith was strengthened because she had to believe in order to conceive. Hebrews 11:11 confirms it: "By faith Sarah herself also received strength to conceive seed, and she bore a child when she was past the age, because she judged Him faithful who had promised."

Scripture's account of Sarah presents an important lesson. We often need help with *apistia*, or a lack of faith. The Lord provided strength for Sarah. He helped her even without her request; how much more, then, will He strengthen us when we ask? In January 1991, I was touched by the father's plea in Mark 9, and I prayed for a stronger faith that Daddy would become a Christian. I prayed and waited. God answered.

That September, my sister, Donna, was diagnosed with leukemia and needed a bone marrow donor. Daddy was the only family member whose blood antigens matched hers. He was 62 years old but eager to help in the medical procedure that might save her life. While praying for Donna, I continued to pray for Daddy. In January 1992, while waiting for the transplant, Donna pleaded, "Daddy, I may not make it. I want to know that I will see you again in heaven." Daddy was baptized that very hour. My husband had the privilege of baptizing him. I do not believe God caused Donna's illness, but He – who makes "all things work together for good" to those who love Him (Romans 8:28) – helped this circumstance to move Daddy's heart. Donna died later that year in August. Her faith has become sight, and she awaits the rest of our family to join her – including Daddy.

Whatever you are praying for, don't give up. Wait on the Lord. First John 5:14-15 tells us, "[T]his is the confidence that we have in Him, that if we ask anything according to His will, He hears us. And if we know that He hears us, whatever we ask, we know that we have the petitions that we have asked of him." Nick Hamilton, in a 2001 Freed-Hardeman University lecture, observed, "To become impatient and allow faith and hope to wane is a serious mistake made by many. God neither wears a watch nor owns a calendar. He is a being of eternity, not confined to time. When he speaks, he has every option of fulfilling his word at any time and in any way he chooses. Our task is to wait on him."[34] This is true.

When Sarah learned this lesson, she was able to conceive and bear the son God promised Abraham. When I learned this lesson, I was able to see my earthly father become a spiritual child of our heavenly Father. God does not always answer yes to our requests, but His Word teaches that "without faith it is impossible to please Him, for He who comes to God must believe that He is, and that He is a rewarder of those who diligently seek Him" (Hebrews 11:6). Let us remember the lesson Sarah learned. If our faith is weak, we must ask for strength. God will help our unbelief. Wait on the Lord.

Reflection Questions

1. List Sarah's godly traits and her weaknesses shown in this lesson. Why does Scripture emphasize her faith and not her doubt?

2. Discuss the common attitudes about conception in Sarah's day and how they affected her decision to "rent" Hagar's womb.

3. What consequences resulted from Ishmael's birth?

4. This lesson includes several authors' quotes concerning the importance of waiting on God's timetable. Choose one, and explain how it applied to Sarah's life.

5. Consider Rosemary McKnight's statement, "Our waiting has a purpose." Share your personal experiences in God's waiting room.

Spiritual Exercise

Share this lesson with someone who is struggling in "God's waiting room" today.

Chapter 8

Enlightening Solitude
Hagar

Genesis 16:1-16; 21:1-21

Jennifer, a recent Christian convert, had been in a hopeless condition. Her broken marriage and torn family made her feel like a failure. She recounted her spiritual state at that time: "I needed God, but I didn't know who He was. I knew *of* Him, but I didn't *know* Him." She was willing to listen when Mary Beth approached her with the gospel. Jennifer was elated to learn the truth about God. At her baptism she began a relationship with Him that has changed her life!

This lesson is about a woman in Scripture who also found herself in a hopeless condition. Hagar was Sarah's handmaid, the one used to bear Abraham's first child. She, too, found God and regained hope in life. Genesis 16:3 describes her as "the Egyptian." She may have been procured while Abraham and Sarah were in Egypt during the Canaanite famine (Genesis 12:14-16).

We noted in our last lesson that Sarah waited years for God's promise of a child, but she finally gave up. She urged Abraham to "go in to" Hagar so that she might have children and build up Sarah's dynasty (Genesis 16:2). The biblical text reveals that Sarah gave Hagar "to her husband Abram to be his wife" (v. 3).

Instead of consulting God, Abram yielded to his wife's suggestion, and Hagar conceived. As George Van Pelt Campbell warns,
"Human schemes that depart from God's ways often backfire
and produce bitterness and suffering."[1] This was the result of
the couple's faithless actions.

The Scriptures' Message

The biblical account turns the spotlight on Hagar in Genesis
16:4: "And when she saw that she had conceived, her mistress
became despised [became little[2]] in her eyes." Hagar became
filled with self-importance. Thomas Whitelaw proposes an as-
sumption by Hagar that because God had rejected Sarah, perhaps Abraham would, too, and she (Hagar) might be elevated to
Sarah's position. Thus, Hagar, "immediately on perceiving her
condition, became insolent (Proverbs 30:23)."[3] Katherine Cook
has imagined the scene this way: "[A]fter Hagar conceived, she
began to gloat and flaunt her condition before Sarah, making
her feel like a dried-up old prune. ... Sarah was forced to watch
as her greatest wish, to bear her husband's son, was granted to
another woman."[4]

Of course, Sarah would not tolerate Hagar's egotistical attitude.
Ancient customs legally entitled a mistress to do as she pleased
with her servants.[5] But Sarah had given Hagar to Abraham as
a "secondary wife."[6] Whitelaw observes that with passionate
irritation and regret, Sarah sought Abraham's permission for
"thrusting her back into the condition of a slave."[7] This was legal
under Sumero-Babylonian law, which stated: "If she has given a
maid to her husband and she has borne children, and afterward
that maid has made herself equal with her mistress, because she
has borne children her mistress shall not sell her for money; she
shall reduce her to bondage and count her among the female
slaves."[8] Sarah wanted Hagar out of the picture.

A wife has tremendous influence on the husband who loves
her. Just as Abraham yielded to Sarah's scheme to lie with Hagar,
he now yielded to her jealous plea to demote her:

Then Sarai said to Abram, "My wrong be upon you! I gave my maid into your embrace; and when she saw that she had conceived, I became despised in her eyes. The LORD judge between you and me." So Abram said to Sarai, "Indeed your maid is in your hand; do to her as you please." And when Sarai dealt harshly with her, she fled from her presence (Genesis 16:5-6).

James C. Okoye explains, "In giving Hagar as wife to Abram, Sarah had transferred authority over her to Abram. ... The response of Abram was to strip Hagar of the status of secondary wife and to hand her back to Sarah."[9] Sarah demoted Hagar; but she went even further in punishment. According to Whitelaw, her harsh treatment probably involved "stripes or maltreatment of some sort."[10] Beatings would have brought Hagar to the point of intolerance. She therefore lived up to her name – from the Arabic term for "flight" – by running from her mistress and heading back home to Egypt. The route she traveled ran from Hebron past Beersheba, and she stopped "by the spring on the way to Shur" that is east of Egypt (Genesis 16:7; 25:18).

The purpose for Hagar's journey was to escape abuse, but it had an even better ending. On the way she encountered "the Angel of the LORD" (Genesis 16:7). Scholars suggest that this was actually "the incarnation of the God-Man" and "the same Lord who appeared to Abraham."[11] Hagar, alone and in the wilderness, met the Lord.

Scripture shows solitude to be a good setting in which to develop a relationship with Him. Jesus sought such quiet times to be alone with God. He spent 40 days and 40 nights alone in the desert before His temptations by Satan (Matthew 4:1-2). Before choosing His twelve apostles, He spent an entire night alone on a mountain in prayer (Luke 6:12-13). After He had heard that John the Baptist had been beheaded, Jesus departed by boat into a desert place to be alone (Matthew 14:10-13). After feeding the 5,000, He sent the multitudes away and went up into a mountain alone to pray (v. 23). After teaching and healing great multitudes, Jesus withdrew to be alone in the wilderness to pray (Luke 5:15-16). And in the Garden of Gethsemane, He withdrew from His disciples to kneel in prayer (22:41). Jesus spent time alone with God – not just in times of crisis or when contemplating important decisions – but also for daily spiritual refreshment. Jan Johnson observes:

> Some may wonder why Jesus would need a pattern of private getaways while living on earth as a human being. Hadn't he already spent eternity in fellowship with the Father? This puzzled even the disciples, who are portrayed in the Gospels as having to find Jesus when he had gone away to pray. People have said he did it primarily to set a marvelous example for us today. But his urgency and frequency hint at something better – he sought solitude simply because he longed to be alone with God.[12]

If Jesus needed such quiet times alone with God, how much more do we? Mark 6:31-32 explains that He urged His apostles, " 'Come aside by yourselves to a deserted place and rest a while.' For there were many coming and going, and they did not even have time to eat. So they departed to a deserted place in the boat by themselves." Jesus knew the value of solitude for communion with God. He made it a regular practice.

How often do you spend time alone with God? Do you let the busyness of life hinder solitude with the Father? He urges us: "Be still, and know that I am God" (Psalm 46:10). Richard Foster suggests that some people actually avoid stillness and quiet:

> Our fear of being alone drives us to noise and crowds. We keep up a constant stream of words even if they are inane. We buy radios that strap to our wrists or fit over our ears so that, if no one else is around, at least we are not condemned to silence. T.S. Eliot analyzes our culture well when he writes, "Where shall the world be found, where will the word resound? Not here, there is not enough silence."[13]

Obviously, Hagar did not withdraw to be alone with God intentionally. She may have heard about Him only through conversation with Abraham and Sarah. Hagar had no clue that God had a life-changing interest in her. The biblical text reveals their conversation in the wilderness:

> The Angel said, "Hagar, you are Sarai's servant. Why are you here? Where are you going?" Hagar said, "I am running away from Sarai." The Angel of the Lord said to Hagar, "Sarai is your master. Go home to her and obey her." The Angel of the Lord also said to Hagar, "From you will come many people. There will be so many people that they cannot be counted." The Angel of the Lord also said, "Hagar, you are now pregnant, and you will have a son. You will name him Ishmael, because the Lord has heard that you were treated badly, and he will help you; Ishmael will be wild and free, like a wild donkey. He will be against everyone. And everyone will be against him" (Genesis 16:8-12 ETRV).

It was only during Hagar's time alone with God that she realized His involvement in her life. In solitude – listening and responding to His words – Hagar became personally aware of Him whom she called "You-Are-the-God-Who-Sees" (Genesis 16:13). She thought, "I see that even in this place God sees me and cares for me!" (v. 13 ETRV). Solitude provides a fertile atmosphere in which to commune with God. This exercise aids in developing spiritual maturity.

Jacob (Abraham's grandson) had a similar experience. He was fleeing from his brother's threat of murder when he stumbled upon the presence of God in an unplanned hour of solitude (Genesis 28:10-16).[14] Interestingly, just as the Lord promised Hagar, Jacob too would be blessed with descendants too numerous to count (vv. 13-15). His reaction reveals a transformed heart:

> Then Jacob awoke from his sleep and said, "Surely the LORD is in this place, and I did not know it." Then Jacob made a vow, saying, "If God will be with me,

and keep me in this way that I am going, and give me
bread to eat and clothing to put on, so that I come back
to my father's house in peace, then the LORD shall be
my God (vv. 16, 20-21).

Scripture gives no indication of Hagar's spirituality before her
encounter with the Lord. But it does suggest that by spending
time alone with Him – listening to Him and talking with Him
– she developed faith in Him. She realized His mercy through
His promise to bless Ishmael, the son in her womb. Hagar also
learned about her child's future, that his descendants would
always dwell in the presence of her mistress's descendants (Genesis 16:10-12). Corinne S. Elkins has commented, "The enmity
between the Arabs and the Jews only heightens each day. Never
was a promise more true than when God told Hagar in verse 12
that Ishmael would be a wild man, his hand would be against
every man and every man's hand would be against him." [15]

Hagar believed in God and submitted to His instructions to
return to Sarah. Her flight plan was changed, and so was she.
Spending time with God does this to people. Okoye suggested
that God "apparently saved Hagar from her rebellious self and
restored Abram's child to him." [16] It appears that she was able to
restrain herself from insolent behavior and remain with Sarah
for about 15 more years.

Soon after her return, "Hagar bore Abram a son; ... Abram
was eighty-six years old when Hagar bore Ishmael to Abram"
(Genesis 16:15-16). Hagar felt blessed. Did she, like Sarah, believe
this child was the fulfillment of God's promise to Abraham?
Even Abraham maintained this belief. When he was 99 years old
(and Ishmael was 13), the Lord reaffirmed the covenant promise
(Genesis 17:1, 25). In this conversation, Abraham exclaimed, "Oh
that Ishmael might live before You!" (v. 18). God responded,

No, Sarah your wife shall bear you a son, and you shall
call his name Isaac; I will establish My covenant with
him for an everlasting covenant, and with his descendants after him. And as for Ishmael, I have heard you.

> Behold, I have blessed him, and will make him fruit-
> ful, and will multiply him exceedingly. He shall beget
> twelve princes, and I will make him a great nation. But
> My covenant I will establish with Isaac, whom Sarah
> shall bear to you at this set time next year (Genesis
> 17:19-21).

The next year Sarah bore Isaac. This child of promise displaced
Ishmael in Abraham's household, but bitterness remained in
Sarah's heart. We get a glimpse of the family relationship in
Genesis 21:8-11:

> And Abraham made a great feast on the same day
> that Isaac was weaned. And Sarah saw the son of
> Hagar the Egyptian, whom she had borne to Abra-
> ham, scoffing. Therefore she said to Abraham, "Cast
> out this bondwoman and her son; for the son of this
> bondwoman shall not be heir with my son, namely
> with Isaac." And the matter was very displeasing in
> Abraham's sight because of his son.

Sarah would no longer accept Ishmael in the home. She urged
Abraham to cast out Hagar and "her son." Okoye suggests that
the term "cast out" here is a technical term for the putting away
of a wife by the husband; hence, "Sarah is forcing Abraham to
divorce Hagar … and revoke his adoption of Ishmael."[17] Abraham loved Ishmael. He did not want to throw him out. This time,
therefore, he sought God's counsel. If he had done this originally
before going in to Hagar, the whole problem would have been
avoided (Proverbs 3:6). God answered Abraham's plea:

> But God said to Abraham, "Do not let it be displeas-
> ing in your sight because of the lad or because of your
> bondwoman. Whatever Sarah has said to you, listen to
> her voice; for in Isaac your seed shall be called. Yet I
> will also make a nation of the son of the bondwoman,
> because he is your seed." So Abraham rose early in
> the morning, and took bread and a skin of water; and

putting it on her shoulder, he gave it and the boy to Hagar, and sent her away. Then she departed and wandered in the wilderness of Beersheba (Genesis 21:12-14).

When their water was gone, Hagar lost hope. She left Ishmael under a shrub and distanced herself from him. Genesis 21:16 reveals that she sat down about a "bowshot" away from him because she could not watch him die. Then she "lifted her voice and wept." Here, for the second time, Hagar found herself alone in the wilderness. But this time she was not rebelliously heading back home to Egypt. This time she sat crumpled in a heap of rejection and sadness, weeping in helplessness. She was concerned about the welfare of her son. While in this solitude, was she seeking the "God-Who-Sees"?

The Maturity-Building Discipline of Solitude

Biblical solitude may be defined as "complete aloneness for spiritual purposes."[18] We have noted that Jesus demonstrated such withdrawal to spend time with God. We, too, should take time to be alone, study, pray, and seek God's will in our lives. It would be presumptuous to say that Hagar in her escape in Genesis 16 purposefully sought solitude. She was not seeking God, but He appeared to her nevertheless. Hagar responded to His instructions and returned to her mistress.

In her second solitude experience (Genesis 21), Hagar also unexpectedly encountered God. Abraham had received divine permission to heed Sarah's request and to cast Hagar out. Thomas H. Leale points out that Hagar did not run away; she was "driven out by a Divine decree."[19] It turned out to be a good experience.

"Times of solitude," writes Adele Calhoun, "can be sweet times, but they can also be dark times when God seems to remain withdrawn and silent."[20] Hagar and Ishmael ended up in the wilderness alone and helpless. Perhaps you've been there. Sometimes God removes the "hedge" around human beings – as He did in Job's case (Job 1:9-12) – and allows us to experience deep, dark valleys:

physical pain, a lengthy illness, financial crisis, concern for a lost loved one, or other seemingly insurmountable circumstances.

Such rough times may last a few hours, a few days, or they can stretch into months and years. Israel experienced many years of God's apparent absence as they suffered in Egypt. God also seems conspicuously absent in the book of Esther. Read the laments of the psalmists who asked, "God, where are you?" (Psalms 10:1; 13:1; 42:9; 44:23-24; 74:1; 88:14). The most touching lament was Jesus' cry, "My God, My God, why have You forsaken me?" (Matthew 27:46).

God has told us, "I will never leave you nor forsake you" (Hebrews 13:5). But His presence must not be taken for granted. Eugene Peterson suggests that the times when He seems absent are "necessary to prevent us from reducing God Almighty to god-at-my-beck-and-call."[21] This reminds me of a story about a little girl in a grocery store. She kept trying to let go of her mother's hand in order to explore the store alone. Finally, her mother released her to be alone. It wasn't long before the little girl became lost and sought again her mother's comforting hand. Fourth-century contemplative St. John of the Cross gave a name to this difficult and confusing period when God seems far away: "the Dark Night of the Soul."[22] It is not a biblical term, but it defines the experience. Foster encourages,

> When God lovingly draws us into a dark night of the soul, there is often a temptation to seek release from it and to blame everyone and everything for our inner dullness. The preacher is such a bore. The hymn singing is too weak. The worship service is so dull. We may begin to look around for another church or a new experience to give us "spiritual goose bumps." This is a serious mistake. Recognize the dark night for what it is. Be grateful that God is lovingly drawing you away from every distraction so that you can see him clearly. Rather than chafing and fighting, become still and wait.[23]

Some of our dark nights involve concern for loved ones. A Christian sister found out that her son had an addiction problem. She suffered in agony because he would not seek help. Her heart was broken, and she felt completely helpless. Like Hagar, this mother simply could not bear to watch her child languish. She sought God's help through prayer in solitude. She asked for a strengthened faith. In time her prayers were answered, and her story had a happy ending.

When we, like Hagar, find ourselves drawn unwillingly into such dark trials, we must trust that God has His purposes. Meanwhile, He wants us to take time to be alone with Him for prayer and study. Trust during dark times produces spiritual maturity (James 1:2-4).

Understanding the concept of solitude from the biblical perspective is important. Robert L. Plummer warns that if the Bible is not our basis for understanding any spiritual exercise, "we will be in danger of adopting non-Christian religious practices or others' experiences as the basis for our supposed Christian spirituality."[24] Eastern forms of solitude (meditation) are examples of such misconceptions. They stress the need to become detached from the world, "to be freed from the burdens and pains of this life and to be released into the impersonality of Nirvana" or to "merge with the Cosmic Mind."[25] The purpose for biblical solitude is to detach from wickedness and distractions of the world in order to develop greater attachment to God. Did this happen to Hagar? Had she developed a relationship with the "God-Who-Sees"?

Benefits of Hagar's Solitude: Deliverance and Her Dynasty

Scripture does not reveal Hagar's level of spirituality after her first solitude experience. We do not know whether she prayed to Him after that encounter. Perhaps she did. Maybe she leaned on Him during those trying times of serving Sarah and gained strength to hold her tongue when she wanted to scream, "I am the mother of Ishmael, Abraham's son. You placed me in this situation! Do not treat me unjustly!" She did believe in God. Her second trip into solitude demonstrates that believers are not immune to life's dark valleys.

During this second experience, Hagar was alone in the wilderness and completely helpless. Leale suggests that this feeling of helplessness is necessary for transformation; only when man has "exhausted all his resources" can God appear and bring help.[26] Perhaps prayer was involved when Hagar "lifted her voice and wept" (Genesis 21:16). God again comforted Hagar: "God heard the voice of the lad. Then the angel of God called to Hagar out of heaven, and said to her, 'What ails you, Hagar? Fear not, for God has heard the voice of the lad where he is' " (v. 17). There was no need for Hagar to fear. God had promised He would take care of Ishmael (16:10-12; 21:12-13). Hagar's fear expresses faithlessness, the same trait exhibited by her mistress Sarah, who would not wait on the Lord.

But the same "God-Who-Sees" was still in control. He said to Hagar, "Arise, lift up the lad and hold him with your hand, for I will make him a great nation" (Genesis 21:18). He delivered them during this second solitude experience. The water Abraham had given Hagar was gone. But "God opened her eyes, and she saw a well of water" (v. 19). Was this refreshing well of water there all the time? Had Hagar failed to see it in her state of desperation? Leale proposes,

> Providence gave her the power to use natural resources. No unnecessary miracle is wrought .... He who knows and controls the thoughts of all men imparts directing ideas, and teaches men rightly to employ the resources already given. That Power which gives us to see what was before hidden, and rightly to employ it, helps us most effectually.[27]

How often do we miss obvious solutions to our problems? Scripture provides answers we often fail to see because we do not seek His Word on the matter. Calhoun has commented, "Alone, without distractions, we put ourselves in a place where God can reveal things to us that we might not notice in the normal preoccupations of life." [28]

God kept the promises He had made to Hagar during her earlier solitude. Ishmael became a great nation: "So God was with the lad; and he grew and dwelt in the wilderness, and became an archer. He dwelt in the Wilderness of Paran; and his mother took a wife for him from the land of Egypt" (Genesis 21:20-21). He and Isaac together buried Abraham in the cave of Machpelah, where Sarah was also buried (23:19; 25:9). Ishmael bore "twelve princes" and lived to be 137 years old (vv. 12-18). It was Ishmael's descendants who purchased Isaac's grandson, Joseph, from his brothers and transported him to Egypt (37:28).

Hagar engaged in two solitude experiences. During the first she met the Lord, and during the second – Leale states – she "obtained her freedom." [29] God fulfilled His commitment to her son, and Isaac and Ishmael separated into two distinct nations. Leale further explains:

> Ishmael was to form a nation by himself, and it was therefore necessary that he should leave the family of Abraham .... The fortunes of a great nation were at this moment depending upon a weak and perishing lad. Thus, from small and insignificant beginnings (as they appear to us) God works His way to the accomplishment of the great things of human history. [30]

Solitude offers opportunity for quiet times with God, which aids in developing spiritual maturity. In her solitude, Hagar became "a changed woman." [31] This describes many today who find God and come out of hopeless situations. Jennifer, the recent Christian convert mentioned at the beginning of the chapter, would agree. In her desperate condition she was open to learn His true identity. Hagar too became personally aware of the "God-Who-Sees." James 4:8 tells us, "Draw near to God and He will draw near to you." We should not wait for crisis situations or trials to meet Him. We can become close to our heavenly

Father every day by spending time, listening and responding to His words – in solitude.

Reflection Questions

1. What was Hagar's attitude after Ishmael's conception? How did Sarah respond?

2. Why did God allow Abraham to cast out Hagar (Genesis 21)?

3. Read again the Scripture texts noted in this chapter concerning Jesus' times alone with God. Do you find such need for solitude?

4. Compare Hagar's two solitude experiences (Genesis 16 and 21).

5. Have you endured a "dark night of the soul" period? What resources did you discover that you never noticed amid the normal preoccupations of life?

Spiritual Exercise

Create a place for solitude. Jesus had a special place to withdraw (Luke 22:39; John 18:2). Create a quiet and lovely area in your home for regular prayer and Bible study. Suggestions: A corner of the bedroom, a swing on the front porch, or a nook in the kitchen may work well.

Chapter 9

Challenging Suffering
Naomi

Ruth 1:20-21

The northwest doors of our church building open to a beautiful garden created in memory of three young people: Jackson, Andrea and Jeffrey. Their parents are still heartbroken. It isn't natural to bury your children. Time, by itself, does not always heal. After the funeral parents can become bitter. Harriet explained to me her grief in the loss of her son:

> We chose to become better. At first we had so much support that gave us peace. God was with us. But later I hit a wall. People quit talking about Jeff, and I felt it was a nuisance to share my feelings. After two years I should have been strong, but I became bitter and angry. I went to counseling and learned that anger is a natural part of the process. Now I'm in a good place. My son was an active Christian. We'll see him again. I'm better.

Naomi of the Old Testament went through a similar process after she lost two children and her husband. Scripture emphasizes her initial bitterness. But through the love of a daughter-in-law, a near kinsman and some concerned neighbors, Naomi learned to rejoice in God again.

The Scriptures' Message

Naomi's story is found in the Bible book named for her daughter-in-law, Ruth. Ruth was a Moabite who played an important role in the history of God's people. Studies about this book often focus on Ruth; however, some see Naomi as the main character. Brian Weinstein suggests:

> Naomi is the central actor in the Book of Ruth. The book explains her mission, which is to lead Ruth to the land of Judah and to have her marry Boaz. The union of Ruth and Boaz begins a process that culminates in the birth of David. As monarch, David will change Israel from its decentralized, weak, and sometimes chaotic, rule under the judges to centralized, powerful, and orderly rule under the monarchy." [1]

We will not debate the centrality of Naomi's role. We will simply examine her life – not to present a God-ordained plan to bring Ruth out of Moab, but to show that God can take a shattered life (even self-imposed bitterness) and create from it a rich, providence-drenched outcome that furthers His divine purpose.

Like Hannah, Naomi lived during the time of the judges when "everyone did what was right in his own eyes" (Judges 21:25). A famine came upon Israel. In Scripture, famines often were the result of God's intentional action as either a punishment for disobedience or a test that required faith. [2] If this famine occurred to test Israel's trust, Naomi's family failed.

Her husband, Elimelech, moved them out of Bethlehem ("house of bread") to seek food in the country of Moab (Ruth 1:1-2). Historically, Israel had a bad relationship with this pagan nation. The Moabites originated from an incestuous relationship between Lot and his daughters back in the days of Abraham (Genesis 19:36-37). Interestingly, Elimelech followed Abraham's example in seeking refuge outside of God (12:10). But Elimelech should have known better. He lived under the Mosaic Law that warned the Israelites to follow God completely, or they would "perish among the nations, and the land of your enemies shall eat you up" (Leviticus 26:27, 38).

And that's what happened. Elimelech, whose name means "boastful and arrogant," died in Moab (Ruth 1:3). Naomi became a widow and was left in this foreign land with their two sons: Mahlon ("sickness") and Chilion ("pining").[3] Both men took Moabite wives: Chilion married Orpah, and Mahlon married Ruth (Ruth 1:4; 4:10); and although they remained in Moab 10 years, no children are mentioned. Some suggest that curses pronounced upon the disobedient (Deuteronomy 28) fell upon this family, leading to the boys' poor health (vv. 65-66), marriage to foreign wives (v. 32; 7:3-4) and infertility (28:18). What heartache Naomi endured! Peter W. Coxon suggests that, in Bethlehem, Naomi was "surrounded by empty stomachs" and in Moab "by empty wombs."[4]

Then the unthinkable happened: "[B]oth Mahlon and Chilion also died" (Ruth 1:5). Naomi lost everything. She was now not just a widow but a "widow indeed" – the biblical term for a woman with no means of support (1 Timothy 5:5 KJV). Naomi was in Moab and away from her physical and spiritual family who cared for widows (Deuteronomy 24:19-21). How did she handle this chaos in her life? Did she pray? Did she take comfort in God's Word? Scripture reveals none of her thoughts – until her decision to return to Bethlehem.

Naomi received word that God was again blessing Israel; the famine had ended (Ruth 1:6). She headed homeward, and her daughters-in-law began with her. But for some reason Naomi stopped and urged them, "Each of you should go back home to your mother. You have been very kind to me and my dead sons. So I pray the Lord will be just as kind to you. I pray that he helps each of you to find a husband and a nice home" (vv. 8-9 ETRV). As they cried and refused to leave, Naomi reminded them that Israel's Levirate marriage law was not feasible:

Turn back, my daughters; why will you go with me? Are there still sons in my womb, that they may be your husbands? Turn back, my daughters, go – for I am too old to have a husband. If I should say I have hope, if I should have a husband tonight and should also bear sons, would you wait for them till they were grown? Would you restrain yourselves from having husbands? No, my daughters; for it grieves me very much for your sakes that the hand of the LORD has gone out against me! (vv. 11-13).

Orpah decided to go back home. Naomi urged Ruth also to go "back to her people and to her gods" (Ruth 1:15). Why would she encourage them to return to idol worship? This first glimpse into Naomi's heart shows her perspective regarding these tragic events. Although her name meant "pleasant, gentle," this woman, worn down by tragedy, had become fatalistic and bitter toward God. A lack of faith shows in her excuse: "The hand of the LORD has gone out against me!" (v. 13).

But in reality, Naomi was blessed with a kind, caring and supportive daughter-in-law. Ruth's memorable "oath of allegiance" to Naomi is often cited in weddings:

Entreat me not to leave you, Or to turn back from following after you; For wherever you go, I will go; And wherever you lodge, I will lodge; Your people shall be my people, And your God, my God. Where you die, I will die, And there will I be buried. The LORD do so to me, and more also, If anything but death parts you and me (Ruth 1:16-17).

Ruth's response was actually a vow. Numbers 30:9-11 explains that a widow's vow was a solemn pledge. To violate it would bring a curse. Some suggest this is why Naomi gave up the argument and allowed Ruth to accompany her.[5]

As scene two of this narrative opened, Naomi and Ruth had arrived in Bethlehem (Ruth 1:19). The women of the city noticed Naomi's changed appearance in her 10 years of absence.

James Morison, in *The Pulpit Commentary*, writes that "on both the wayfarers the finger-marks of poverty, involuntary signals of distress, would be unconcealable."[6] The women asked, "Is this Naomi?" (v. 19). The "pleasant" turned "bitter" widow retorted, "Do not call me Naomi; call me Mara, for the Almighty has dealt very bitterly with me. I went out full, and the LORD has brought me home again empty. Why do you call me Naomi, since the LORD has testified against me, and the Almighty has afflicted me?" (vv. 20-21). Did Naomi really go out full? Her family left Bethlehem to find food. Did she really come back empty? She brought with her a loving and loyal daughter-in-law. Ronald T. Hyman describes the returning-home scene:

> By chiding the women, Naomi establishes her intention not to be too neighborly and friendly. She is bitter and lets everyone know it. The exchange with the women of Bethlehem also allows Naomi to reject her identity. In the preceding verses, Ruth has taken a crucial step toward changing her identity. Here, Naomi stands in contrast to Ruth by rejecting her family-given name. She does not want to be called Naomi (pleasant); she requests the women to call her Marah (bitter). Naomi is rejecting and bitter; Ruth is accepting and hopeful.[7]

Much like Hagar in the desert, Naomi felt hopeless. For her, life was over. She would never again smile. Yet Naomi had an advantage over Hagar; she had been born and raised among God's people. Naomi had opportunity to develop faith and trust in Jehovah. But it appears she had not. She was like one "raised in the church" who never cultivated her personal faith. She had taken God's blessings for granted, and when difficulties came, she blamed Him. Trials of life happen to each of us. We have a choice to become bitter or better.

The Maturity-Building
Discipline of Patience in Suffering

When sin entered the world, so did suffering – both physical and emotional. Such life challenges include chronic pain and illness, guilt, anger, coping with death and grief, stress and depression. With these trials comes the temptation to give up and let them destroy you. James reminds us that "the testing of your faith produces patience" (James 1:3). He explains to those who would blame God: "Let no one say when he is tempted, 'I am tempted by God'; for God cannot be tempted by evil, nor does He Himself tempt anyone" (v. 13).

Satan is the author of suffering. When Adam and Eve listened to him, the result was hard labor in the field and in childbearing (Genesis 3:16-17). When God removed the hedge around Job and allowed testing, it was Satan who caused his losses and pain (Job 1:9-19; 2:7). Listen to Job's spiritually mature response: "God gives us good things, and we accept them. So we should also accept trouble and not complain" (2:10b ETRV). Job endured his troubles with God's help; afterward, "the LORD blessed the latter days of Job more than his beginning" (42:12).

Of course, enduring suffering is easier said than done. Christian counseling can help one better understand the natural processes involved in suffering. For those dealing with the death of a loved one, for example, Granger E. Westberg offers help in his book, *Good Grief*:[8]

STAGES OF GRIEF

1. We are in a state of shock: "I can't believe this has happened."

2. We express emotion: "It hurts so very much. I weep."

3. We feel depressed and very lonely: "Does anyone care? I'm so alone."

4. We may experience physical symptoms of distress: "I become physically and emotionally ill."

5. We may become panicky: "I feel like I'm losing my mind!"

6. We may feel a sense of guilt about the loss: "Why didn't I do more for my beloved?"

7. We are filled with hostility and resentment: "Why did God do this to me? Why did the doctor do what he did?"

8. We are unable to return to usual activities: "We carry all the grief within us by ourselves."

9. Gradually, hope comes through: "We begin to re-enter life and find meaningful experiences again."

10. We struggle to affirm reality: "We believe God helps us to face the present and the future. With hope based on God, we can live and love again."

When we understand the natural processes involved in suffering, we are able to view our troubles from God's perspective. Then they become not only bearable but beneficial. The Easy-to-Read Version presents James' words in an encouraging way:

My brothers and sisters, you will have many kinds of troubles. But when these things happen, you should be very happy. Why? Because you know that these things are testing your faith. And this will give you patience. Let your patience show itself perfectly in what you do. Then you will be perfect and complete. You will have everything you need (James 1:2-4).

Paul echoes this concept: "And we are also happy with the troubles we have. Why are we happy with troubles? Because we know that these troubles make us more patient. And this patience is proof that we are strong. And this proof gives us hope" (Romans 5:3-4 ETRV). The Greek term translated "patience" means "endurance, steadfastness, perseverance." This involves enduring adversity without giving up. The trait of "patience" is named among the seven virtues we must add to our Christian faith (2 Peter 1:5-6 KJV).

We can determine for ourselves how we handle life's difficulties. My friend Vickie Ramsey Greenway is a breast-cancer survivor.

She wrote a lighthearted book called *Humor 'n' Healing* to encourage women enduring this trial. In it she says, "Life is ten percent what happens to us and ninety percent how we deal with it." [9]

An inspirational story that has appeared in church bulletins and on the Internet illustrates various responses to trials. Titled "Carrots, an Egg and Coffee Beans" and attributed to Mary Sullivan, the story involves a conversation between a wise mother and her "trial-enveloped" daughter. The mother puts three pots of water on the stove to boil. She then places some carrots in one pot, an egg in another and some coffee beans in the third.

After 20 minutes they examine each pot. The carrots, which had been strong and unrelenting, had become soft and weak after enduring the boiling water. The fragile, "thin-skinned" egg had become hardened on the inside. But the coffee beans had a unique outcome: They had changed the water. Each of the items had been subjected to the same circumstance – boiling water – but each reacted differently.

The mother asks her daughter to consider her response to adversity. Does she, like the carrots, lose strength and wilt? Or, like the egg, does her spirit become bitter and tough? Or is she like the coffee bean, which – in harsh circumstances – releases its fragrance and flavor? The daughter, hopes her mother, will decide to become like the coffee bean.

We've all heard axioms that echo the same message: "People are like tea bags. God sometimes puts them in hot water to see how strong they are." And another: "Are you like a thermometer or a thermostat?" The thermometer reacts to its surroundings, letting the circumstances control it. The thermostat does not allow its surroundings to have that power. It controls the atmosphere around itself.

James wrote, "Is anyone among you suffering? Let him pray" (James 5:13). With God's help we can be like the coffee bean, the tea bag and the thermostat. We can come out of difficult circumstances better. Naomi began to count her blessings when she patiently endured her suffering and praised God.

Benefits of Naomi's Patient Suffering: A Pleasant Attitude and a Legacy

Naomi had not endured her suffering with patience. She did not trust God to make all things work together for good (Romans 8:28). Like Hagar, her despair was needless. God had provided the means for her life restoration (Ruth); but, like Hagar, Naomi didn't see it. When she returned to God's people, her eyes were opened and things began to change.

It was "the beginning of barley harvest" (Ruth 1:22). The edges of the fields were left for the orphans, widows and poor (Deuteronomy 24:19-21). Ruth offered to gather grain to support Naomi and herself. The field in which she gleaned belonged to Boaz, one of Elimelech's relatives. Boaz was the son of Rahab, the harlot of Jericho who converted to Jehovah (Matthew 1:5).[10] When Boaz learned that Ruth was Naomi's daughter-in-law, he offered her grain and protection with the workers in his fields (Ruth 2:8-16).

Naomi's heart was touched. She praised God for His kindness to her and to Ruth and also to their dead husbands (Ruth 2:20). Naomi also realized that Levirate marriage could be the means for her dead husband's land to be redeemed! C.F. Keil observes:

> In the case before us Elimelech had possessed a portion at Bethlehem, which Naomi had sold from poverty (4:3); and Boaz, a relation of Elimelech, was the redeemer of whom Naomi hoped that he would fulfill the duty of a redeemer, namely, that he would not only ransom the purchased field, but marry her daughter-in-law Ruth, the widow of the rightful heir of the landed possession of Elimelech, and thus through this marriage establish the name of her deceased husband or son (Elimelech or Mahlon) upon his inheritance.[11]

The "near kinsman" extension of Levirate law allowed the nearest relative to marry the widow of a deceased man. Then the dead man's house could be "built up" (Deuteronomy 25:5-10). Interestingly, Naomi did not mention the Levirate law until after the harvest was over (Ruth 2:23; 3:1-2). Was she afraid Boaz might refuse and turn them away? Or did it take time for the love and kindnesses of Ruth and Boaz to melt Naomi's heart and move her to suggest the idea?

Opinions vary regarding Naomi's attitude in this matter. Read different translations of Ruth 3:1. How should we understand Naomi's statement, "My daughter, maybe I should find a husband and a nice home for you. That would be good for you" (v. 1 ETRV)? Lottie Beth Hobbs asserts that Naomi was unselfish, thinking of Ruth's welfare in 1:8-13.[12] But some view her motives skeptically. Keil suggests that she stated literally, " 'It is my duty to seek for thee' ... a peaceful and well-secured position."[13] Morison proposes that after the harvest, Naomi immediately made the case for the "matured scheme in her head."[14] We do not know how much Naomi's heart had changed during the short harvest season. Perhaps Naomi was still bitter. Time is required for the grief process to produce hope.

But in this scene Naomi instructed Ruth to initiate a Levirate marriage proposal. She urged her to wash, change clothes, go down to the threshing floor where Boaz was winnowing barley, wait until he lay down, then uncover his feet and ask him what she should do.[15] Charles P. Baylis suggests that Naomi's instruction (to put on her "best garment") was not according to Hebrew tradition and God's law, for the mourning clothes "identified her legal position as a widow."[16] Tamar wore the widow's attire for many years (Genesis 38:11-14). Keil concurs that Naomi misunderstood Levirate law. He and Baylis explain that such legal proceedings were to be transacted publicly at the city gate in the daytime, not "by a well-relaxed man and an appealing woman alone on a threshing floor in the darkness of night."[17] Such a scheme was carried out by Lot's daughters (19:30-38).

But let us assume Naomi meant well in her aggressive matchmaking. Ruth obeyed her mother-in-law (Ruth 3:6-14). Boaz was flattered that she would ask him to accept the role of "kinsman-redeemer" (NIV). But he informed her about a closer relative. Boaz proceeded according to the Mosaic covenant by calling a public meeting at the city gate. Read 4:1-12. The nearer kinsman refused to take on the responsibility of "kinsman-redeemer." Therefore, Boaz took off his shoe to show his acceptance of Elimelech's property and of Ruth as his wife. The "shoe" ceremony is explained by Morison, "When they took possession of property, they planted the foot on the newly acquired soil, an outward expression of taking possession of it, and asserting a right to it."[18]

Boaz married Ruth, and they had a son (Ruth 4:13). What a happy ending! Brian Weinstein observes, "Ruth had to wait to be married to Boaz in order to give birth. God kept her barren for the 10 years of her marriage to Naomi's son, just as he kept Sarah, Rachel and Hannah barren for years after their marriages. His reason in the case of Ruth is that He wanted her to give birth in Judah to ensure Jewish identity for her offspring."[19]

The son was a blessing – but not only to Ruth. Naomi's life was restored. This woman, whose name meant "pleasant," may have begun life as a happy child who dreamed of marrying her Prince Charming and living happily ever after. Perhaps life was pleasant when she married and bore two sons. However, marriage to "arrogant" and caring for "sickness" and "pining" amidst people who "did what was right in their own eyes" may have required more maturity that Naomi possessed. Imagine moving to a foreign country and then losing all your family! Without a deep faith and trust in God, no wonder Naomi became bitter.

However, when she returned home to God's people, things changed. Naomi witnessed love and kindness from a precious daughter-in-law, a compassionate "near kinsman," and concerned women in her community. Baylis concludes, "Before her return Naomi experienced the curses God had promised. But from the point of her return onward (Ruth 2–4) Naomi received the physical blessings promised in the Mosaic covenant, namely food and children."[20] When the child was born to Boaz and Ruth, Naomi "took the boy, held him in her arms, and cared for him" (Ruth 4:16 ETRV). The women of Bethlehem celebrated with her, declaring, " 'There is a son born to Naomi.' And they called his name Obed" (v. 17). He would become the father of Jesse and grandfather of King David.

God promises to bless us when we remain close to Him. This is made possible by staying involved in His church and surrounded by Christian brothers and sisters. There we find support in our sufferings and happiness in our joys (Romans 12:15). Lives can be restored. This is what happened to Naomi. The women of Bethlehem rejoiced with her and proclaimed, "Blessed be the LORD, who has not left you this day without a close relative; and may his name be famous in Israel! And may he be to you a restorer of life and a nourisher of your old age; for your daughter-in-law, who loves you, who is better to you than seven sons, has borne him" (Ruth 4:14-15). Morison provides a tender summary of Naomi's blessed end:

> The story of Ruth closes amidst domestic prosperity and happiness, and amidst neighborly congratulations. And it is observable that Naomi, whose trials and sorrows interest us so deeply at the commencement of this book, appears at its close radiant with renewed happiness. … She is encompassed with the blessings which, in the language of our poet, "should accompany old age" – "honor, love, obedience, troops of friends." [21]

Naomi learned to endure patiently her suffering. Through all of the right processes, her bitterness and anger disappeared. She had God and good people with her; like Harriet, the grieving mother we met at the beginning of the chapter, she could say in the end, "I'm in a good place now."

Reflection Questions

1. Do you consider Naomi or Ruth more central to this study's biblical account? If so, why?

2. Discuss activities by Elimelech and Naomi that demonstrated a lack of faith.

3. In what ways was Ruth a blessing to Naomi's life?

4. How did Naomi's time of endurance differ from Sarah's "waiting room"?

5. Share a challenge in your life for which you suffered. Did you endure it with patience and trust in God? What were the results?

Spiritual Exercise

Do something special for someone who is suffering after a loved one's death or is struggling with a difficult illness, such as cancer. Greenway writes, "The smallest good deed is better than the greatest intention."[22] Here are some of her suggestions:[23]

1. Call and say, "I'm going to the store. Do you feel like making out a shopping list, or do you want me to guess what you need?"

2. Call and say, "My gift to you is that I'm either cleaning your house or having it cleaned – my treat. What is your preference?"

3. Bring food – especially food that doesn't have strong aromas.

4. Send an uplifting card or handwritten note.

5. Visit, but make the visits short so that you don't tire the loved one.

6. Make quick "how are you?" phone calls.

7. Call someone going through something similar to what you have endured, and offer to answer questions or share information that you've gathered.

8. Rent a movie for someone recuperating from illness. Pick it up and return it.

9. Give a book especially chosen for the patient to help pass the time.

10. Let someone know you are praying for him or her, and have that person on other Christians' prayer lists.

11. Strive to lighten the load by creating laughter.

Chapter 10

Courageous Faith
Jochebed

Exodus 2:1-10; Hebrews 11:23

*N*ancy is a most unique member in our congregation, known for her deep Southern accent, her skill as a sharp-shooter, her conservative political views, and her remarkable trust in God. When her son, an Air Force pilot, participated in eight tours in Iraq, Nancy's faith kept her heart strong. She prayed, "Lord, I've done all I can do. He's in your hands. Take care of him."

The time comes when every mother must release her children. Like Nancy, most have the opportunity to raise them and teach them needed lessons for a good life. But some must let go much too early, as Hannah did. The Old Testament reveals the account of another mother who released her son – when he was just 3 months old.

This mother was a Hebrew named Jochebed (which means, "Yahweh is glory"). Her son, in his adult years, would proclaim Yahweh as the God of glory (Leviticus 9:6). Jochebed is unnamed in our text but is later identified as the wife of Amram, her brother's son (Exodus 6:20). They had two older children: a daughter, Miriam, and 3-year-old Aaron (Numbers 26:59).

The Scriptures' Message

It was a tragic time in Israel's history, when every male child came into the world "with a death sentence on his head."[1] The Hebrews had been in Egypt about 400 years when a new Pharaoh came to power "who did not know Joseph" (Exodus 1:8). Joseph was the son of Jacob (Israel), who brought his family to this land and whose numerous descendants seemed a threat to Egypt. The worried Pharaoh took steps to slow their birthrate. First, he burdened them with hard work. But this only increased their numbers (vv. 9-12). Then he issued an edict for the midwives to kill all newborn Hebrew males as they were delivered upon the "birthstool" (a special chair with a hole in the seat; v. 16).

However, the midwives feared God. They did not obey Pharaoh's edict but allowed the babies to live (Exodus 1:17). They gave the excuse that the Hebrew women were more "lively" (vigorous) than Egyptian women and able to deliver themselves before the midwives arrived (v. 19). It was, therefore, too late to kill them at birth.

Like Rahab, these women obeyed God rather than the pagan king. It is always right to "obey God rather than men" (Acts 5:29). And, like Rahab, they were rewarded. Exodus 1:20-21 reveals, "God dealt well with the midwives … . He provided households for them." George Rawlinson, in *The Pulpit Commentary*, explains,

> He blessed them by giving them children of their own, who grew up and gave them the comfort, support and happiness which children were intended to give. There was a manifest fitness in rewarding those who had refused to bring misery and desolation into families by granting them domestic happiness themselves (2 Samuel 7:11; Ruth 4:11).[2]

Pharaoh must have been a rather weak man. There is no evidence that he punished the midwives. He was not even dignified with a name in Scripture. But God honored the two midwives by placing their names in Exodus 1:15: Shiphrah ("elegant, beautiful") and Puah ("one who cries out").[3] These two women did what was right through passive resistance of the evil edict. Terence E. Fretheim has commented:

These women are not leaders of the community, persons in a position of influence who could have an impact on governmental policy. Yet such persons are not powerless. In the process of carrying out their rather mundane responsibilities they are shown to have had a profound effect on the future of their people. God is able to use persons of faith from even lowly stations in life to carry out the divine purpose. Moreover, there is no indication in the story that this courageous activity ever becomes public; it could easily have been forever lost amid all the movements of kings and nations. But the deeds of these women are made known somehow, and their names remembered, while the king of Egypt in all his pomp and splendor remains forever nameless.[4]

Pharaoh's scheme did not work, so he made a final decree, charging Israel, "Every son who is born you shall cast into the river, and every daughter you shall save alive" (Exodus 1:22). Little did he know that as he was planning the extermination of the Hebrew nation, "God was planning their emancipation."[5] That same Nile River, in which so many Hebrew babies died, would serve as the place where the future deliverer of Israel would be saved.

That future deliverer was the infant son of Jochebed and Amram. But the royal edict dictated that he be thrown into the Nile. Jochebed faced a dilemma similar to what some face today. Many years ago I knew a young woman who learned through an ultrasound that her baby had no legs. Her husband would not accept this child and convinced her to abort. Reluctantly, she did. Even after a memorial service with her Christian friends, she could not forget the tiny baby she had carried for six months. Guilt plagued her. She knew that God hates "[h]ands that shed innocent blood" (Proverbs 6:16-17). Human life is sacred.

Jochebed saw that her baby was "a beautiful child" (Exodus

2:2). She would not toss him into the Nile, so she hid him. The term for "hid" carries the sense of "treasuring and protecting something of great value."[6] As we can imagine, at 3 months old this precious treasure became difficult to hide. Jochebed made a papyrus-reed (wicker) basket and covered it with "asphalt and pitch" to make it waterproof. Then she placed her child in this "ark" (floating box) and set it among the bulrushes by the bank of the Nile. These papyrus plants, at 10 to 15 feet tall, kept the little basket from floating away.

What went through this mother's mind as the ark and its precious cargo floated among the reeds? She probably prayed, like Nancy, "Lord, I've done all I can do. He's in your hands. Take care of him." Jochebed's action was an "exercise of faith!"[7] Hebrews 11:23 reveals that it was "[b]y faith" that Moses' parents hid him three months "because they saw he was a beautiful child; and they were not afraid of the king's command." Because "faith comes by hearing and hearing by the word of God" (Romans 10:17), we know that some Hebrews practiced God's laws while in Egyptian bondage. Jochebed obeyed God by courageously acting like the midwives; that is, she passively resisted the edict. Fretheim asserts, "The preservation of the lives of these babies takes priority over the murderous edict of a very important and powerful person, even at the risk of their own lives."[8] What a lesson for us today!

Jochebed's baby was not left unattended. His sister watched to see what would happen to him. This sister is also unnamed here, but we assume it was Miriam. She stood afar off so that no one would guess she was related to the mother who had disobeyed Pharaoh. Miriam was ready to respond to the person who found her little brother. Scripture explains what happened:

> Then the daughter of Pharaoh came down to bathe herself at the river. And her maidens walked along the riverside; and when she saw the ark among the reeds, she sent her maid to get it. And when she opened it, she saw the child, and behold, the baby wept. So she

had compassion on him, and said, "This is one of the Hebrews' children." Then his sister said to Pharaoh's daughter, "Shall I go and call a nurse for you from the Hebrew women, that she may nurse the child for you?" And Pharaoh's daughter said to her, "Go." So the maiden went and called the child's mother. Then Pharaoh's daughter said to her, "Take this child away and nurse him for me, and I will give you your wages." So the woman took the child and nursed him (Exodus 2:5-9).

Most likely, Pharaoh's daughter came regularly to bathe at this place. Perhaps she had talked with the Hebrew women and children and Jochebed had observed her kindness. As Miriam watched, the Egyptian princess saw the basket, asked her handmaid to get it and opened it herself. How surprised she must have been to find a baby! And how fitting that he should begin to cry. Joseph S. Exell suggests that his tears were a "fit emblem of his nation's grief."[9] Had Pharaoh's daughter felt compassion for the Hebrews under her father's tyranny? When she saw that this child was Hebrew, she may have realized why he was abandoned. No loving mother could throw this adorable infant into the Nile. Perhaps she chuckled to herself to think, as John I. Durham cleverly suggests, that this is "exactly where Hebrew boy-babies were supposed to be cast" and, therefore, it seems his mother did obey "the Pharaoh's grim command."[10]

Did this Egyptian princess wonder at the "coincidence" of a Hebrew maiden coming so quickly to suggest a wet nurse? Did she wonder if Jochebed was the mother? Or did God providentially blind her to such thoughts? All we are told is that "the baby wept. So she had compassion on him" (Exodus 2:6). Rawlinson observes, "At once her woman's heart, heathen as she was, went out to the child – its tears reached the common humanity that lies below all differences of race and creed – and she pitied it."[11] The princess could not kill this child.

God was in control. He delivered Jochebed's baby because of her faith and because He needed a future deliverer for Israel.

Pharaoh's daughter fit right into God's plan. According to Cindy Colley, she had no idea she "was about to become a tool in the hand of a Workman whose precision and purpose cannot be thwarted. She was about to become a piece in the puzzle of propitiation. She, in fact, was about to bring home the baby who would eventually bring down the kingdom!"[12] Not even Jochebed knew this. She just trusted God.

Pharaoh's daughter appears to have had her weak daddy wrapped around her little finger. She was not afraid to defy his law. She even adopted this child as her own. Fretheim suggests that this "public demonstration of the bankruptcy of his policy" may have diffused the threat for other Hebrew sons.[13] Scripture does not tell how long the edict remained in effect. It may have continued for years and diminished the number of males close to Moses' age. All we know is that in a dangerous time for Hebrew baby boys, Jochebed's son was saved. She trusted God.

The Maturity-Building Discipline of Trust

Proverbs 3:5-6 tells us, "Trust in the LORD with all your heart, And lean not on your own understanding; In all your ways acknowledge Him, And He shall direct your paths." When Jochebed realized she was pregnant, what were her first thoughts? She probably had witnessed the grief of other mothers losing their newborn sons. Did she hope for a girl? A faithless woman may have resigned herself to the inevitable. Like Hagar, she might have hidden her face, unable to watch the fate of her son. But Jochebed trusted in the Lord with all her heart.

We learned in our lesson about Dorcas that "faith without works is dead" (James 2:20). Hebrews 11 lists many Old Testament men and women who demonstrated faith in action. These include Abel's sacrifice (v. 4), Noah's ark (v. 7), Sarah's conception (v. 11), Abraham's offering (vv. 17-19), Rahab's hiding of the spies (v. 31), and Jochebed – again, unnamed – listed in verse 23 as acting "[b]y faith." Verse 1 gives a definition: "Now faith is substance of things hoped for, the evidence of things not seen." Faith acts when there is no obvious solution. Faith is trusting God.

A good example of faith appears in the movie *Raiders of the Lost Ark*. Indiana Jones stands at the edge of a deep chasm; the only way of escape is to believe that a path of stepping stones will appear as he jumps. Peter showed faith when he stepped out of the boat and walked on water (Matthew 14:29). It is what the Israelites did when they walked by faith across the Red Sea on dry land (Exodus 15:19). It is what Sarah did when she engaged "in the intimacy of the marriage bed"[14] and "By faith ... received strength to conceive seed ... when she was past the age, because she judged Him faithful who had promised" (Hebrews 11:11). By faith Jochebed hid her child and, after seeing God's protection during those three months, she trusted that He would watch over him in the ark – and in his future.

Trust is required in our Christian walk. Satan is doing his best to undermine our faith. Educators teach evolution; but Hebrews 11 assures us, "By faith we understand that the worlds were framed by the word of God, so that the things which are seen were not made of things which are visible" (v. 3). By faith we can know that God keeps His promises (Titus 1:2), that He is with us (Matthew 28:20), and that He will reward us with eternal salvation (2 Timothy 4:8; Revelation 2:10). Paul reassured the Christians in Romans 5:1, "Therefore, having been justified by faith, we have peace with God through our Lord Jesus Christ." Jochebed, like my friend Nancy, was a mother who trusted God and had peace concerning her son.

Benefits of Jochebed's Trust: Salvation for a Son and a Nation

In her dilemma, Jochebed acknowledged God's power. She released her son into His hands by placing him in the little basket among the reeds. Like Hannah, she was willing to "forgo the joys of raising him."[15] But God, "who is able to do exceedingly abundantly above all that we ask or think" (Ephesians 3:20), rewarded her faith. He not only delivered her child from harm, but allowed Jochebed to have him back. Coy Roper writes, "It is remarkable that, because of the sister's suggestion, Moses' mother was able to nurse him, feeding him at her own breast. More than this, she was paid to do it!"[16]

Jochebed was blessed to continue mothering her son: rocking him to sleep in the arms to which he was accustomed, singing his favorite lullabies, laughing with his happy coos, and kissing away his tears, thankful for every precious moment. How wonderful to see her faith rewarded this way – but she knew her time with him would end too quickly. He would be weaned soon.

While Jochebed nursed, rocked and sang to her baby, her son "sat at the feet" of his mother. Like Hannah, Jochebed taught her son about God and the responsibility to wholly follow Him. These godly mothers show us the importance of those first few years. A dear sister in Christ I knew died when her son was only 4 years old. His father did not raise him in the Lord, but the boy remembers his mother's God and her hymns of praise. Those seeds will bear fruit. Christian young women, consider the possibility that the father of your children may raise them without you.

Jochebed also instilled in her son an understanding of his Hebrew identity, as a transplant in the ungodly land of Egypt. Exell observes,

> Who could better teach him the wrongs of his country than she – that hundreds had suffered the fate he had managed to escape – the slavery of his people – the tyranny of the king – and that during the most sensitive time of his life. His mother instructed him during the earliest days of his youth – her instruction would, therefore, be enduring – hence he would go to the Egyptian court with a knowledge of his country's woe – and of his father's God.[17]

This interesting observation teaches several things about child-rearing. Mothers (and fathers) must be diligent in their children's spiritual training. Satan works through worldly activities and relationships to draw them away from God. A few hours a week in Bible class are simply not enough to ensure a foundation of godly principles. Jochebed's precious child, decades later, would declare to Israel God's prescription for spiritual training:

> And these words which I command you today shall be in your heart. You shall teach them diligently to your children, and shall talk of them when you sit in your house, when you walk by the way, when you lie down, and when you rise up. You shall bind them as a sign on your hand, and they shall be as frontlets between your eyes. You shall write them on the doorposts of your house and on your gates (Deuteronomy 6:6-9).

My husband and I took this scripture literally. In the evenings I enjoyed reading Bible stories to our children. Steven taught them when we "rose up." He showered the boys and blow-dried their hair while reciting the books of the Bible and their themes.

Jochebed and Amram taught their children. Little did they know that they also were preparing Miriam to lead the women of Israel and Aaron to be the first high priest. William J. McRae writes about their youngest child, Moses: "His initial training came from godly parents who laid a spiritual foundation and sowed the spiritual seed. God was even training and preparing Moses for his ultimate calling."[18] The faith his parents instilled in him worked to make this man a great servant-leader in biblical history.

When Jochebed fulfilled her wet-nurse obligations, the time came to give up her child – again. Exodus 2:10 begins, "And the child grew, and she brought him to Pharaoh's daughter, and he became her son." The Egyptian princess formally adopted this child and named him Moses, explaining, "Because I drew him out of the water." This name in its Hebrew form (*mosheh*) means "to draw out (from the water)."[19] R. Alan Cole suggests that she, most likely, knew the Hebrew language because "an Egyptian mistress might well understand and use the tongue of her domestic servants to give orders."[20]

Jochebed could not have released her son to a pagan without believing God was in control. Fretheim points out that "it takes faith, 'the conviction of things not seen' (Hebrews 11:1 NASB), to perceive that God is at work."[21] Parents, do not fret. What appears to be a hopeless situation may actually be filled with possibilities. Our friend Gary Washer was raised in a Christian home. He rebelled and became a drunk and a drug addict. Something happened in his life that turned him around, and he now teaches others how to overcome addiction. His seminars through the church are titled "Removing Emotional Pain" (www.sftaware-ness.org). Exell is right to encourage, "Let parents do their best for the safety of their children – physically – morally – in wisdom – and Providence will find the means for their temporal – and eternal rescue – education – destiny."[22]

God had a plan for Moses. Stephen's martyrdom sermon gives a historical overview:

> But when the time of the promise drew near which God had sworn to Abraham, the people grew and multiplied in Egypt till another king arose who did not know Joseph. This man dealt treacherously with our people, and oppressed our forefathers, making them expose their babies, so that they might not live. At this time Moses was born, and was well pleasing to God; and he was brought up in his father's house for three months. But when he was set out, Pharaoh's daughter took him away and brought him up as her own son. And Moses was learned in all the wisdom of the Egyptians, and was mighty in words and deeds (Acts 7:17-22).

Moses was instructed in all the wisdom of the Egyptians. As Exell stated, "Providence placed him in the best school of the day,"[23] for, during that time, Egypt was the very seat of learning. Among the subjects taught were grammar, history, medicine, arithmetic, geometry, astronomy, engineering, archaeology, reading and writing the hieroglyphic script, the copying of texts, instruction in writing letters and formal documents, learning the languages and geography of Canaan, and studying contemporary codes of law (e.g., Hammurabi's).[24] Imagine the usefulness of such information in dealing with the responsibilities that lay in Moses' future. As McRae observes, "Pharaoh paid the bill for an education beyond the means of Amram, but in doing so he gave Moses the training which was indispensable to his ministry. God was preparing Moses for the authorship of the Pentateuch, his leadership of Israel, and his administration of the Mosaic covenant and legal code."[25]

In addition, Moses witnessed firsthand the inner workings of Egyptian leadership. This was valuable experience for one who would, 80 years later, stand before a Pharaoh and present God's message to let His people go. Exell proposes:

Hence the discipline of the court was as necessary to his future and usefulness as that of the school. In the palace he saw, in all its force, the tyranny of the king – the degradation of Israel – and the prowess of the nation he would have to combat. This, pre-eminently, was the school of his life, and he was made its scholar by Providence. ... When heaven undertakes the education of a life – it does so thoroughly and completely."[26]

What a wonderful example Jochebed models for Christian women today. She obeyed God's law and, "by faith," hid her child for three months. Then she let him go. She put him in the little ark and waited for God to work. You can almost hear her pray, like my friend Nancy, "Lord, I've done all I can do. He's in your hands. Take care of him." Exell beautifully summarizes Jochebed's role:

[W]hen all her means of self-help were exhausted, then she gave him into the Divine care. So, as a rule, God does not educate the children of indolent parents. He moves in the line of the mother's best effort. When she has done her best – put him on the river – not forgotten him – prays for him – then God will send Pharaoh's daughter to save, and educate the boy.[27]

Jochebed solved her dilemma by trusting God. Perhaps she lived to see Moses follow her example by aligning himself with God. He developed his own faith. Hebrews 11 lists him among the Old Testament heroes: "By faith Moses, when he became of age, refused to be called the son of Pharaoh's daughter, choosing rather to suffer affliction with the people of God than to enjoy the passing pleasures of sin" (vv. 24-25).

Moses was not the son of Pharaoh's daughter. He was the son of Jochebed. She taught him well during the few years he was with her. Moses grew up to fulfill God's plan as the deliverer of Israel. He boldly stood and proclaimed the glory of Yahweh. An entire nation reaped the blessings God showered upon Jochebed. She was a godly mother who trusted God.

Reflection Questions

1. Discuss the decisions Jochebed made when her son was 3 months old.

2. Do you know anyone who has had an abortion? What other options were available?

3. Discuss instances of God's providence in Moses' life.

4. Have you faced a problem in which no visible solution forced you to step out on faith? Share your experience.

5. Discuss the importance of early spiritual training of children.

Spiritual Exercise

Gather a list of questions from young mothers about the spiritual training of children. Enlist a panel of four godly grandmothers ("older women," Titus 2:3-5), and provide a class session for the sharing of biblical and practical advice.

Chapter 11

Thanksgiving Worship
Miriam

Exodus 15:20-21

The saying, "Those who wish to sing always find a song," may bring to mind certain women in your congregation. In my congregation we think of Teresa. She is a songwriter for country music artists in Nashville. Perhaps you have heard her lyrics to "Country Ain't Country," sung by Travis Tritt. Many women live with a happy tune on their lips. Christian women focus some of their songs on worship to God.

In previous lessons we noted two thanksgiving songs: Mary's Magnificat (Luke 1:46-55) and Hannah's Song (1 Samuel 2:1-10). This lesson will examine a brief "victory hymn" in which Miriam led the women after Israel's deliverance from Egypt.[1]

The Scriptures' Message

Miriam was the eldest child born to Jochebed and Amram. Scholars describe her as a bright, happy, ingenious, loving girl, wise beyond her years.[2] She was the unnamed sister who watched as Pharaoh's daughter found baby Moses among reeds in the Nile (Exodus 2:4-8). Scripture does not say whether Miriam was prompted by her mother; but she approached the princess, asking,

"Shall I go and call a nurse for you from the Hebrew women, that she may nurse the child for you?" (v. 7). Miriam demonstrated that same spirit of service 80 years later when she led the Israelite women in praise to God.

Miriam's Song appears at the end of a Hebrew poem about God's deliverance at the Red Sea (Exodus 15:1-21). The entire poem is known in Judaism as Shirat ha-Yam, "The Song of the Sea."[3] John I. Durham proposes that this song was "stimulated by an exceptional moment in Israel's history."[4] Israel had just witnessed God's power through the 10 plagues and the parting of the Red Sea, walked across the seabed on dry land, and watched the complete destruction of Egypt's pursuing army (14:21-29). Their response is summarized in verse 31: "Thus Israel saw the great work which the LORD had done in Egypt; so the people feared the LORD, and believed the LORD and His servant Moses."

Standing on the other side of the Red Sea, the multitude felt overwhelmed with awe and thanksgiving. They raised their voices in praise (Exodus 15:1-21). Durham observes that this poem is "not comparable to any one psalm, or song or hymn, or liturgy known to us anywhere else in the OT [Old Testament] or in ANE [Ancient Near Eastern] literature."[5]

This special song is presented in two parts. The first is called "The Song of Moses," for it includes the words of Moses and the children of Israel (Exodus 15:1-19). The last two verses (vv. 20-21) present the women's words led by Miriam. The poem was structured antiphonally; that is, two groups sang the words alternately to one another, and the women's part reinforced the thanksgiving of the entire group.[6] Four suggestions have been offered to explain how it was sung. Nahum M. Sarna, editor of *The JPS* [Jewish Publication Society] *Commentary*, presents three: (1) "the people repeated or completed the phrase or verse that Moses initiated"; (2) "the verses were recited by them in alternation"; and (3) "the people recited the entire song after Moses had finished it."[7] Coy Roper adds a fourth: "One more possibility is that Miriam and the women sang the chorus (v. 21) after each line or two."[8]

Exodus 15:1 begins the song: "Then Moses and the children

of Israel sang this song to the LORD, and spoke, saying, I will sing to the LORD, for He has triumphed gloriously! The horse and its rider He has thrown into the sea!" Verses 2-19 record the body of the praise hymn. In verse 21 we find repetition in Miriam's joyous acclamation: "Sing to the LORD, For He has triumphed gloriously! The horse and its rider He has thrown into the sea!" Both parts follow a reference to the destruction of the Egyptian army at the Red Sea. Moses' song follows the Exodus 14:21-29 account. Miriam's song follows the account of the scene of Moses' song.

Verse 20 records the first mention of Miriam's name. The name's root forms – Miriam, Mary and Marah – all suggest "bitterness." Bitter Naomi had asked the women of Bethlehem to call her Marah. Miriam's later life reflected this meaning; but here, in response to the mighty acts of God, she joyfully led the women in praise. She is introduced as "the prophetess, the sister of Aaron." Aaron was a prophet serving as Moses' spokesman (Exodus 4:10-16; 7:1-2). Such individuals were "raised up by God and inspired by His Spirit to proclaim His will and purpose."[9] Miriam was the first prophetess named in Scripture, but some others followed: Deborah (Judges 4:4), Huldah (2 Kings 22:14), Noadiah (Nehemiah 6;14), the woman in Isaiah 8:3, and Anna (Luke 2:36).

It is important to note that Miriam and Aaron were under the divinely ordained leadership of Moses. Keil and Delitzsch have pointed out that even though Miriam was Moses' deliverer in his infancy, she occupied "in the congregation of Israel, namely, as ranking, not with Moses, but with Aaron, and like him subordinate to Moses, who had been placed at the head of Israel as the mediator of the Old Covenant."[10] In directing the women in song, Miriam followed Moses.

Let's examine the manner in which the women engaged in their song of praise. Miriam "took the timbrel in her hand; and all the women went out after her with timbrels and with dances" (Exodus 15:20). Singing with timbrels and dances was common in Jewish history. A timbrel was a tambourine (hand drum), a wood or metal hoop about one hand's-breadth wide and covered with leather.[11] Such instruments were common in Egypt, generally played by women, and continue to be a favored instrument in Eastern festive and sacred occasions.[12]

In Old Testament celebrations, timbrels were usually accompanied by dancing. The psalmist urged, "Praise him with the timbrel and dance" (Psalm 150:4). Jephthah's daughter came out "to meet him with timbrels and dancing" (Judges 11:34). After David killed Goliath, the women of Israel came out "singing and dancing ... with tambourines" (1 Samuel 18:6). Roper observes, "Dancing was a way of expressing joy in ancient times."[13] This was not the sexually stimulating reveling of some modern dances. Joseph S. Exell has described Jewish female dance from the letters of Lady Mary Wortley Montague in which "the great lady" was "followed by a troop of young girls who imitate her steps. If she sings, they make up the chorus."[14] Miriam led the Israelite women in this way with timbrels and dance. At the Red Sea they proclaimed the powerful faithfulness of God.

The Maturity-Building Discipline of Worship in Song

Miriam models for us joyful thanksgiving worship in song. Her own lyrics began, "Sing to the LORD" (Exodus 15:21). David also encouraged, "Sing to God, you kingdoms of the earth; Oh, sing praises to the Lord" (Psalm 68:32). God enjoys hearing us sing to Him. Scripture instructs us, "Communicate to each other with psalms, hymns and spiritual songs. Sing and make music in your hearts to the Lord" (Ephesians 5:19 ETRV).

Singing to God must not spring merely out of obligation. Our praise should be a response to His goodness and sovereignty. Read Psalm 63:1-5, in which the seeker thirsted to satisfy his soul. He could not find fulfillment in this "dry and thirsty land" (v. 1). When he experienced God's lovingkindness, he burst into song: "My lips shall praise You. Thus I bless You while I live; I will lift up my hands in Your name. My soul shall be satisfied as with marrow and fatness, And my mouth shall praise You with joyful lips" (vv. 3-5). Jehovah is God! And He is mindful of us (Psalm 8:4). Roper observes that Israel acknowledged this at the Red Sea:

> Moses and the Israelites praised the Lord in song – for who and what He is, and for what He had done by destroying the Egyptian army in the sea. The song depicts the Lord as Israel's strength, song and salvation (Exodus 15:2); He is a warrior with majestic power, who in His anger overthrows His enemies (vv. 3, 6, 7). Furthermore, He is the God above all gods, "majestic in holiness," and a wonder-worker (v. 11).[15]

Our songs are an important part of worship. They extol God's sovereignty and goodness. They also serve as an evangelistic tool and a means of teaching and encouraging other Christians. Israel's song was directed to God but also to the wider world. J. Urquhart writes, "It is the work of God's people in every age to prepare a dwelling-place for him where his character is made known, his voice heard, and his love and fear shed abroad."[16] Terence E. Fretheim adds:

> Even more, praise and thanksgiving are finally a matter of witness before all the world. The purpose of all of God's activity remains that which was articulated in [Exodus] 9:16, "and that my name may be declared throughout all the earth" [KJV] ... [T]he reasons for praise relate specifically to God for what God has done and then to God's relationship to those who do not (yet) honor Yahweh.[17]

Israel was successful in this endeavor. Their songs about God's power spread throughout Canaan. As predicted, the Philistines, Edomites, Moabites and Canaanites heard about the destruction of the Egyptian army and feared the Lord (Exodus 15:14-16a). Remember Rahab's acclamation:

> For we have heard how the LORD dried up the water

of the Red Sea for you when you came out of Egypt, and what you did to the two kings of the Amorites who were on the other side of the Jordan, Sihon and Og, whom you utterly destroyed. And as soon as we heard these things, our hearts melted; neither did there remain any more courage in anyone because of you, for the LORD your God, He is God in heaven above and on earth beneath (Joshua 2:10-11).

Spreading the good news through song is effective today. Alice, a new convert, shared with me, "Singing is what led me to baptism. ... It's one way that I connect to God, and I think I connect as much to God in singing as in prayer." Singing promotes relationship with God and aids in spiritual maturity.

Worship in song is also a way for Christians to teach and encourage one another. Paul urged, "Let the word of Christ dwell in you richly in all wisdom, teaching and admonishing one another in psalms and hymns and spiritual songs, singing with grace in your hearts to the Lord" (Colossians 3:16). People who struggle to attend worship often say that when they go, they feel renewed. This is one of the serendipities of song. One afternoon my husband and I attended a funeral. We were running late, and there was little time to gather clothes for an activity planned afterward. I did not have all my "ducks in a row" and was anxious about it on the way to the funeral. However, the beautiful hymns sung there changed my attitude. Exell writes about the encouraging nature of worship songs:

Despondent soldiers on the march have been known to stop and listen to music stealing far over the waters and to be aroused to vigorous effort in the march. Travelers, hearing strains floating from the windows of some palace or mansion, have been cheered to increase their pace homeward. So, saints, as they war or journey, listen to the exultant symphonics poured over the walls and battlements of heaven, and, setting their feet to the measure of the eternal hymn, press onwards

toward the city, within whose fadeless palace halls
shall be sung the everlasting jubilee.[18]

Do certain hymns lift your spirit? The beautiful four-part har-
mony of "The Greatest Commands" urges us to grow in our love
for each other. During the illness and death of my sister, "Does
Jesus Care?" brought me comfort and continues to do so. My
mother-in-law enjoys the communal concept in "God's Family"
and wants it sung at her funeral. "Paradise Valley" helps me focus
on our eternal home. Herbert Lockyer comments about Miriam's
purposeful encouragement: "Miriam sang for God, using her gift
for the elevation of human souls into a higher life. A dreary wilderness faced the children of Israel, and Miriam knew that they
would march better if they sang. So her song was one of cheer and
full of the memory of all God had accomplished for His people." [19]

Like Miriam, in singing we honor God, teach unbelievers and
encourage others. However, her use of timbrels raises questions.
Church historians explain that when the church was established
in the first century, "only singing, however, and no playing of
instruments, was permitted." [20] The style of worship in song
was a cappella, defined by Merriam-Webster as "without instrumental accompaniment" from the Italian phrase *a cappella*,
"in chapel style."

Yes, Old Testament worship included instruments (timbrels,
harp, etc.) as an accompaniment to sacrifices (1 Chronicles 23:5;
2 Chronicles 29:25-28).[21] When sacrifices ended, so did worship
with instruments. Fourth-century writer John Chrysostom wrote
regarding Psalm 149, "In olden times they were thus led by these
instruments because of the dullness of their understanding and
their recent deliverance from idols. Just as God allowed animal
sacrifices, so also he let them have these instruments, condescending to help their weakness." [22] According to New Testament
instructions for worship in song, the melody is to be made in the
Christian's heart (Ephesians 5:19). Second-century theologian St.
Clement of Alexandria proclaimed, "We need one instrument:
the peaceful word of adoration, not harps or drums or pipes

or trumpets."[23] Have you enjoyed the simple beauty of songs exclusively played through godly voices?

Early Christian worship included no mechanical instruments of music. These were added later.[24] *The Catholic Encyclopedia* notes, "For almost a thousand years Gregorian chant, without any instrumental or harmonic addition, was the only music used in connexion with liturgy"[25] The first organ allowed in a New England church was set up in King's Chapel of Boston in 1714 (Church of England).[26] Its introduction came with opposition. It was described as "the devil's bagpipes," an "ensign of Baal," and "a 'popish addition' to the New Testament precedent for the church."[27] Scripture clearly states that music in worship is to be made in the Christian's heart, and with our words we teach and encourage others (Ephesians 5:19; Colossians 3:16). What God desires to hear is a heart with the right spirit and understanding (1 Corinthians 14:15). Therefore, Miriam's use of timbrels does not justify using instrumental music in worship today. What is worthy of imitation is her enthusiastic praise and thanksgiving.

Benefits of Miriam's Worship in Song: Praise to God and Healing

Miriam led the women of Israel in worshipful singing to God. This bright, ingenious older sister to Moses and Aaron was loved by the Hebrew people. She was considered a heroine for her role in Moses' deliverance as an infant and appreciated as a prophetess above the women. God mentioned her leadership role in Micah's prophecy to Israel: "For I brought you up from the land of Egypt, I redeemed you from the house of bondage; And I sent before you Moses, Aaron, and Miriam" (Micah 6:4). Miriam had a spiritually enriching influence in Israel as she followed Moses' leadership and served as a positive role model.

However, it appears that Miriam's gifts of prophecy and singing – which ought to have fostered humility – developed within her an arrogant attitude and led her to criticize publicly Moses, the God-ordained leader of Israel. Moses had been given the power of God's Spirit (Numbers 11:24-25). This was the same Spirit of Jehovah that "came mightily upon David" when he was anointed by Samuel as Israel's future king (1 Samuel 16:13 ESV).

But Miriam became prideful: "Then Miriam and Aaron spoke against Moses because of the Ethiopian woman whom he had married; for he had married an Ethiopian woman. So they said, 'Has the LORD indeed spoken only through Moses? Has he not spoken through us also?'" (Numbers 12:1-2). Lockyer suggests that Miriam criticized Moses out of "patriotic jealousy"; that is, she feared the influence of her younger brother's foreign (Ethiopian) wife.[28] However, her outburst against Moses' leadership signaled rebellion. Keil and Delitzsch assert:

> This elevation of Moses excited envy on the part of his brother and sister, whom God had also richly endowed and placed so high, that Miriam was distinguished as a prophetess above all the women of Israel, whilst Aaron had been raised by his investiture with the high-priest-hood into the spiritual head of the whole nation. But the pride of the natural heart was not satisfied with this. They would dispute with their brother Moses the pre-eminence of his special calling and his exclusive position, which they might possibly regard themselves as entitled to contest with him not only as his brother and sister, but also as the nearest supporters of his vocation.[29]

Perhaps you've caught someone in an unintentional "slip of the tongue." Matthew 15:18 reveals: "But those things which proceed out of the mouth come from the heart." Miriam's actions reflected the root meaning of her name (bitter). Her haughty attitude caused criticism of Moses' marriage and management as Israel's leader.

Moses did not defend himself. He was the baby brother, and he was very humble (Numbers 12:3, "meek," KJV). John Calvin suggested that "he had swallowed the injury in silence, inasmuch as he had imposed a law of patience upon himself."[30] Still, the rebellion needed to be nipped in the bud. The Lord took Aaron and Miriam aside to reaffirm Moses' leadership:

Suddenly the LORD said to Moses, Aaron, and Miriam, "Come out, you three, to the tabernacle of meeting!" So the three came out. Then the LORD came down in the pillar of cloud and stood in the door of the tabernacle, and called Aaron and Miriam. And they both went forward. Then He said, "Hear now My words: If there is a prophet among you, I, the LORD, make Myself known to him in a vision; I speak to him in a dream. Not so with My servant Moses; He is faithful in all My house. I speak with him face to face, Even plainly, and not in dark sayings; And he sees the form of the LORD. Why then were you not afraid To speak against My servant Moses?" So the anger of the Lord was aroused against them, and He departed (vv. 4-9).

God's message was clear. Even Phyllis Trible – who defended the "female voice" in her article "Bringing Miriam Out of the Shadows" – observes, "The divine speech requires little commentary. It answers the issue of leadership and authority by declaring a hierarchy of prophecy. Moses stands peerless at the top."[31]

Miriam and Aaron had challenged Moses' authority. We noted in Chapter 2 that disrespecting God-ordained authoritative roles produces disastrous results. The public criticism of Moses' leadership opened the door for division and rebellion in the camp. Therefore, God judged swiftly. Miriam was stricken with leprosy. Aaron was not. Keil and Delitzsch assert that Miriam acted as instigator and spokesperson because (1) her name appeared first and (2) the Hebrew verb translated "spake" is feminine (Numbers 12:1).[32] R. Winterbotham adds that Aaron "was not the leader in mischief, but only led into it through weakness," a trait already demonstrated in the golden calf incident (Exodus 32:1-5).[33]

For Miriam's rebellion, her skin became "leprous, as white as snow" (Numbers 12:10), that is, a full-blown case of the disease. Aaron saw her pitiful condition "as a still-born child, which comes into the world half decomposed."[34] He asked Moses to intervene:

"Oh, my lord! Please do not lay this sin on us, in which we have done foolishly and in which we have sinned. Please do not let her be as one dead, whose flesh is half consumed when he comes out of his mother's womb!" (vv. 11-12). Moses sympathized. He himself had felt the horror of leprosy as a God-given sign in Exodus 4:6. He pleaded for their sister.

The Lord replied, "If her father had but spit in her face, would she not be shamed seven days? Let her be shut out of the camp seven days, and afterward she may be received again" (Numbers 12:14). Winterbotham notes that God was "thoroughly ashamed" of Miriam's public disgrace and, therefore, gave her an equally disgraceful punishment, adding, "No doubt she had to submit to all the rites there prescribed, humiliating as they must have been to the prophetess and the sister of the law-giver." [35] After a seven-day purification period, Miriam was allowed to re-enter the camp (v. 15). Israel then continued its journey. The people still loved Miriam.

We find nothing more about Miriam until her death in the wilderness of Zin (Numbers 20:1). She was not allowed to enter the Promised Land. Moses spoke about her 40 years later while teaching the Law to a second generation. He warned, "Take heed in an outbreak of leprosy, that you carefully observe and do according to all that the priests, the Levites, shall teach you; just as I commanded them, so you shall be careful to do. Remember what the LORD your God did to Miriam on the way when you came out of Egypt!" (Deuteronomy 24:8-9). Moses admonished Israel not to defy Jehovah's instructions, given through the priests: Rebellion incurs punishment. We do not know whether the song in Miriam's heart returned so that she again praised God. She was given the chance. When we use our God-given talents to His glory – and not ours – He blesses us (Matthew 25:29).

Worship in song is a special maturity-building exercise used to praise God, teach the lost and encourage others. God does not expect perfect voices. He just wants us to make "a joyful noise" (Psalm 100:1 KJV). We express praise and thanksgiving in hymns. Teresa, the songwriter mentioned at the beginning of this chapter, shares her gift of song with others in daily life. She also joins other Christians every Sunday, encouraging the saints in a cappella praise to God. May we humbly participate in thanksgiving praise through worship in song and echo David's joyful words, "I will praise You, O LORD, among the peoples; I will sing to You among the nations" (57:9).

Reflection Questions

1. Read "The Song of Moses" and "The Song of Miriam" in Exodus 15:1-21. Discuss how the entire poem functions as a song of praise.

2. Discuss the reasons given for singing in worship.

3. How might Miriam's role have fostered an arrogant attitude?

4. Why did God strike Miriam with leprosy? Consider Jesus' warning: "Remember Lot's wife" (Luke 17:32).

5. In light of Scripture, compare a cappella singing with the use of instruments in worship.

Spiritual Exercise

Find a book about hymnal backgrounds. Read about some authors and the circumstances that prompted their lyrics. Write out the words of your favorite hymn, and discuss specifically how the words apply to your life.

Aggressive Evangelism
Priscilla

Acts 18:1-3; 24-28

The church includes many evangelistic women. Jean is one example; she has taught home Bible studies together with her husband for more than 50 years. They currently teach the fourth grade Bible class and present the "Now That I'm a Christian" series for new converts. Their outreach follows the example of Priscilla and her husband, Aquila, who together taught the gospel more perfectly to the gifted preacher Apollos. Priscilla remains a godly example of evangelism for Christian women today.

The Scriptures' Message

Priscilla was a career woman who made time for Bible study and evangelism. She is mentioned six times in Scripture. In the Greek text, Paul used her formal name, Prisca (Romans 16:3; 1 Corinthians 16:19; 2 Timothy 4:19). Luke, writing in a more informal style, used the diminutive form (nickname), Priscilla (Acts 18:2, 18, 26). Her Roman name means "worthy" or "venerable."[1] It is possible that she belonged to one of the distinguished families of ancient Rome, such as the gens Prisca family.[2] We do not know whether she was a Jew or Gentile.[3] Scripture identifies only the ethnicity of Aquila: "a Jew ... born in Pontus" (Acts 18:2).

Priscilla and Aquila enjoyed mutual love and respect. Murray J. Harris describes their relationship as "total devotion" and suggested three biblical evidences: Their names always appear together, they worked as tentmakers together, and they left Rome together.[4]

William O. Walker proposes that "the two were so closely associated in the minds of early Christians that reference to one and not the other would have been unthinkable."[5] Aquila's name appears first in Acts 18:2 and 1 Corinthians 16:19. This was the custom of the day. However, in the Greek texts of Acts 18:18, 26; Romans 16:3; and 2 Timothy 4:19, Priscilla is named first. Opinions vary regarding the reason for this. George Knight proposes that it was a matter of Christian courtesy extended to a woman.[6] Harris believes Priscilla may have been better known or had greater visibility because of her giftedness.[7]

We all know couples in which the wife is more outgoing, more active and even more spiritual. We must not assume Priscilla was too assertive or assumed improper leadership (Ephesians 5:22; 1 Corinthians 14:34-35). R.C.H. Lenski writes:

> The beauty of Priscilla's character lies in the fact that she never thrust herself forward, never asserted herself, or made her superiority felt. She was loyally true to Paul's teaching that the husband is the head of the wife. Aquila had found a pearl among women. ... She helped to teach Apollos in all propriety. Since this was private teaching, it in no way conflicted with the apostolic principle that women are to remain silent in the church."[8]

Priscilla was loyal to God and to her husband. This loyalty is seen in their mutual devotion: She left Rome with her husband during banishment of the Jews. Acts 18:2 tells us that Aquila had "recently come from Italy with his wife Priscilla (because Claudius had commanded all the Jews to depart from Rome)." According to first-century historian Suetonius, in his *Life of Claudius*, the Jews were expelled in A.D. 49 in response to "disturbances at the instigation of Chrestus."[9] Christianity was still a relatively new religion, and tension with Judaism caused great turmoil. If Priscilla was a Gentile, Harris observes, she would have been "under no compulsion by reason of race."[10] On the other hand, Dwight L. Moody proposes, "If Aquila and Priscilla were still practicing Jews, this edict would have affected them. If they were already active Christians, this event would indicate that the Jesus movement was considered a sect of Judaism, and thus included in the ban on worship. In any event, Aquila and Priscilla transferred to Corinth."[11] Where Aquila went, Priscilla followed.

In Corinth we see that Priscilla and Aquila worked together as tentmakers (Acts 18:3). Such work was needed in Rome. Pliny the Elder, in his encyclopedic *Natural History*, described the many "awnings of sailcloth" that covered the Roman forum during the hot summers, sky-blue awnings in Nero's amphitheaters, and red awnings used in the inner courts of houses.[12] Harris pointed out that whether or not Priscilla was "a woman of high birth," the fact that she worked with her husband "indicates compatibility and co-operation between the pair."[13]

It is impossible to discuss Priscilla apart from Aquila, for as Herbert Lockyer has stated, "Their two hearts beat as one."[14] Scripture always mentions them together. They left Rome to make a new start in Corinth, which appears to be the first of many uprootings for Priscilla and Aquila. Harris summarizes their mutual devotion: "Rome – Corinth – Ephesus – Rome – Ephesus ... they are always found side by side, toiling at their craft, adjusting to new situations, and creating new circles of friends, always in unison. For them, mutual love and respect as well as marital fidelity were corollaries of being enslaved by Christ."[15] This couple's great relationship is obvious in the fact that they are always mentioned together, working together and traveling together.

Priscilla and Aquila became settled in Corinth – making a living as tentmakers – when they welcomed Paul into their home "because he was of the same trade" (Acts 18:3). It was around A.D. 50, near the end of Paul's second missionary journey. During his mission effort in Corinth, "he reasoned in the synagogue every

Sabbath, and persuaded both Jews and Greeks" (v. 4). We are not told if Priscilla and Aquila were baptized before meeting Paul. Aquila could have been converted by Jews who returned to Pontus after Peter's Pentecost sermon (Acts 2:9). If so, he probably converted Priscilla. Religiously mixed marriages were uncommon in Greco-Roman society. According to ancient literature, it was customary for a wife to worship only the gods her husband worshiped.[16] Scot McKnight notes, "[M]ost scholars are agreed that when a woman struck out on her own and joined a religion different from her husband's, that could be seen as an act of insubordination."[17] Scripture does not give details about when and how Priscilla and Aquila were converted, but they were certainly committed.

Paul stayed in Corinth 18 months, then left for Syria to begin his third missionary journey (A.D. 54-58). Priscilla and Aquila accompanied him (Acts 18:18-19). It would have been difficult to live with Paul a year and a half and not grow in knowledge and passion in the gospel of Jesus Christ. The couple decided to go with him and support his "pioneering evangelism" in Ephesus.[18] Scholars describe their whole-hearted involvement:

> It was a sacrifice for Prisca and Aquila to move again. They lost whatever clientele they had managed to build up in Corinth. But they had started from scratch before, and they knew that they could do it again. And this time they operated under a much more profound imperative than economic survival. The intense involvement … indicates that they had become an integral part of the Pauline mission. All that mattered was the spread of the gospel. Financial loss and personal sacrifice were alike irrelevant.[19]

The three arrived in Ephesus. Paul stayed a short while and then left Priscilla and Aquila while he sailed for Jerusalem and Antioch (Acts 18:21-22). He had confidence that this godly couple would serve as resident missionaries and continue the spread of the gospel in that city.

We know about two specific ministries in which Priscilla and

Aquila were involved while there: They taught the gospel to others, and they opened their home for church assemblies. While Paul was with them in Ephesus, he wrote a letter to the Corinthians (c. A.D. 56). In it he stated, "The churches of Asia greet you. Aquila and Priscilla greet you heartily in the Lord, with the church that is in their house" (1 Corinthians 16:19). Hosting assemblies became a common practice for this couple. Later when they moved to Rome, Paul again greeted them in a letter and "the church that is in their house" (Romans 16:3-5).

This ministry of hospitality has prompted speculation about the couple's lifestyle. Wayne Meeks suggests that their occupation, mobility and residences indicate they were relatively wealthy, independent and middle-class.[20] J. Ernest Runions discussed the cost of time and resources in such hospitality:

> It sounds noble to share, to have the church in the living room. But think of some of the types who came into their living room! That didn't really do much for Aquila and Priscilla's status in society. Imagine the church in your house every Sunday. What would that do to the carpets? Aquila and Priscilla just could not have the church in Ephesus or Rome come in every Sunday without the carpets wearing out and the furniture becoming threadbare.[21]

What dedication! A sister in my congregation has mused, "I wonder if I could cope with a large group meeting in my house every week. As neat as I like to keep my house, it would be a sacrifice to move furniture around and pick up after everyone leaves." For Priscilla it was part of her ministry. There was no church building in which to meet.

It appears that Priscilla opened her home for Bible studies, too. On one occasion she and Aquila took a preacher aside to teach him the gospel more accurately:

> Now a certain Jew named Apollos, born at Alexandria, an eloquent man and mighty in the Scriptures, came to Ephesus. This man had been instructed in the way

of the Lord; and being fervent in spirit, he spoke and taught accurately the things of the Lord, though he knew only the baptism of John. So he began to speak boldly in the synagogue. When Aquila and Priscilla heard him, they took him aside and explained to him the way of God more accurately (Acts 18:24-26).

Apollos was a Jew from Alexandria, Egypt's capital city from 331 B.C. to A.D. 641. It had a large Jewish population and was considered the intellectual center of Christianity at that time.[22] Its large university and library produced great scholars of early Christianity (Clement and Origen), a renowned Jewish-Alexandrine philosopher (Philo), and the Greek translation of the Hebrew Scriptures (the Septuagint).[23] Apollos became eloquent and mighty in the Scriptures. He has been described as "gifted and well-trained dialectically," "powerful/capable," "well-versed in Old Testament writings," and "a devastating debater (cf. Acts 18:28)."[24]

This itinerant preacher was instructed in the way of the Lord. The term "the way" was used to describe Christianity (Matthew 21:32; 22:16; Acts 19:23).[25] He was "fervent in spirit" (18:25). The Greek term for "fervent" means "boil, seethe."[26] This man was on fire for the Lord. Oh, for preachers with such passion today! Lenski beautifully describes his zeal:

> What he had discovered did not appeal to him only intellectually, it captivated his very spirit; he glowed with holy enthusiasm and zeal. He spoke and taught all along (imperfect tenses) what he had learned, *ta peri tou Iasou*, a neat idiom, "the things concerning Jesus" as far as he knew them. He could not keep still about them, he had to impart them also to others; he spoke them to men privately as occasion offered, and he taught them in public, in meetings in the synagogues wherever he happened to be.[27]

Because the synagogue was always open to distinguished orators, Apollos was allowed to speak boldly "the things of the Lord" (Acts 18:25). He knew about Jesus, but was not fully informed.

Luke wrote that, "he knew only the baptism of John" (v. 25). Lenski clarifies, "To know only John's baptism was not to know about the crucifixion, the resurrection, the ascension, Pentecost, etc.; not to know of the Lord's Supper, the first church at Jerusalem, the mission of the apostles, etc."[28] Apollos was teaching what he sincerely believed, but he was "missing out on the most important part of the gospel story."[29] Many eloquent preachers talk about Christ but fail to inform listeners about the whole plan of salvation. Danny Dodds agrees:

> Apollos is representative of so many in our world today who have heard or accepted just part of the story. People who know much but have not heard or accepted the whole gospel story. We need to share our faith with such and make sure they know the rest of the story. That they hear and understand the whole gospel message![30]

Acts 18:25-26 explains that Apollos "spoke and taught (*akribos*) accurately." But "[w]hen Aquila and Priscilla heard him, they took him aside and explained to him the way of God (*akribesteron*) more accurately." If his message was complete, there would have been no need for Priscilla and Aquila to pull Apollos aside to teach him.

Joseph A. Fitzmyer describes Apollos as having "come to a form of Christian faith … a learned orator who speaks accurately about Jesus yet has never heard of Christian baptism."[31] When Paul encountered disciples who knew only about John's baptism, he taught them more accurately (Acts 19:1-5): "Paul said, 'John indeed baptized with a baptism of repentance, saying to the people that they should believe on Him who would come after him, that is, on Christ Jesus.' When they heard this, they were baptized in the name of the Lord Jesus" (vv. 4-5).

Baptism is an essential part of God's plan of salvation. Jesus told His disciples:

Go therefore and make disciples of all the nations, baptizing them in the name of the Father and of the Son and of the Holy Spirit, teaching them to observe all things that I have commanded you; and lo, I am with you always, even to the end of the age (Matthew 28:19-20).

And He said to them, "Go into all the world and preach the gospel to every creature. He who believes and is baptized will be saved; but he who does not believe will be condemned" (Mark 16:15-16).

The Maturity-Building Discipline of Evangelism

In fewer than two decades, our nation has experienced a rise and fall in spiritual hunger. Robert Mulholland wrote in 1993, "Spiritual formation has become one of the major movements of the late 20th century."[32] A 1999 Gallup poll reported that the percentage of Americans feeling the need for spiritual growth surged from 58 percent in 1994 to 82 percent in 1998.[33] This truth was evidenced in television and movies: *Touched by an Angel* (1994-2003), *Beyond Chance* (1999-2000), and *Left Behind* (2000). Then interest began to wane. In 2004, Mel Gibson's *The Passion of the Christ* made a final plea for revival but to no avail. People were turning away from God. A May 2009 *U.S. News & World Report* headline read: "Nonreligious Americans represent the fastest-growing part of the nation's religious landscape."[34] The article revealed that those identifying with no religious tradition, or as atheists or agnostics, accounted for 15 percent of the population, up from about 8 percent in 1990.[35]

Interestingly, the March 2009 *Christian Chronicle* also reported that the church of Christ suffered a 4.7 percent drop between 2003 and 2009.[36] There is a need for evangelism. Runions pleads, "We live in a world hungry for faith. And the only people in the world who can truly meet that need are Christians. We are the only ones with bread of life to fill human emptiness; and God is calling us to share the faith."[37]

Two motivational books about evangelism are *Hearts on Fire* by Don Humphrey and *Evangelizing Your Community* by Dr. Stafford North.[38] Humphrey points to Priscilla and Aquila, urging, "Successful evangelism requires this New Testament kind of boldness!"[39] North discusses the first-century church in Acts: "If we are intent on helping the church today to become more evangelistic, we could have no better starting place than to look at the early church to see (1) how much they grew and (2) how they did it."[40] He provides a 10-point easy-to-understand way to tell the gospel story. Another excellent resource is *Evangelism Made Simple: You Can Do It!* by Stephen Rogers, minister of the Washington Avenue Church of Christ in Evansville, Ind.

My husband, Steven, collected these insights about personal evangelism:

ONE-ON-ONE BIBLE STUDY

Christians are to reproduce after themselves (Matthew 28:18-20). Three considerations must be addressed and established as "givens" at the beginning of a Bible study with someone:

(1) **God is our Creator, and He made us in His image** (Genesis 1:26; Psalm 8; Hebrews 3:4). If your prospect is an atheist, begin with the creation (Psalm 19:1; Romans 1:20). Brad Harrub's book, *Convicted: A Scientist Examines the Evidence for Christianity*, may be helpful.[41]

(2) **The Bible is God's inspired Word** (2 Timothy 3:16-17; 2 Peter 1:20-21; James 1:21-27). If your prospect is not willing to accept the Bible as the inspired Word of God, you may find Neil Lightfoot's book *How We Got the Bible* helpful.

(3) **We are all lost sinners in need of salvation** (Romans 3:23). If your prospects are not convinced they are lost, they will not listen to the Word as seekers, only as observers (Acts 26).

The "good news" (gospel message) is the death, burial and resurrection of Jesus Christ for our sins (1 Corinthians 15:1-4). It is good news because all people break God's law and are separated from Him (Ezekiel 18:20; 1 John 3:4; Romans 3:23; 6:23). Some sins are listed in Romans 1:26-32, Galatians 5:19-21 and Revelation 21:8.

Jesus paid the debt for our sin (Romans 5:6-8; Hebrews 5:8-9), and this free gift of grace is received by baptism into Christ's death (blood; Romans 6:3-4, 17-18; John 19:33-34; Acts 22:16; 1 Peter 3:21). This gospel was preached in the first century and is still preached today (Mark 16:15-16; Acts 2:29-47). Examples of New Testament conversions are found in Acts 2:37-47; 8:27-39; 10:1-48; 16:14-15, 30-34; 18:7-8; 22:12-16. Each convert heard the good news (Romans 10:17), believed in Jesus Christ as the Son of God (John 8:24), repented of their sins (Luke 13:3, 5), confessed faith in Christ Jesus as the Son of God (Matthew 10:32-33), and was baptized for the forgiveness of sins (Acts 2:38; 22:16).[42]

After prospects mentally process these truths and are baptized, they become new converts, born-again babes in Christ (John 3:1-7; 1 Peter 2:2). They need to study first principles (elementary truths from God's Word). Baptism does save us (1 Peter 3:21), but a person can fall from grace (2 Peter 2:20-22). Being a Christian does not mean just being baptized; it is a completely new lifestyle of maturing day by day (Acts 2:42; 1 Corinthians 4:2; Revelation 2:10; Hebrews 10:25; Matthew 25:21, 23). God told us to evangelize – not only so the church may grow, but also so that we ourselves may mature spiritually.

Benefits of Priscilla's Evangelism: A Shared Gospel Message

The biblical narrative reveals two significant concepts: (1) Priscilla and Aquila taught, and (2) Apollos listened. Priscilla took personally God's directive to evangelize. However, she did not violate 1 Timothy 2:11-12. Moody points out that the dialogue took place, not in the synagogue, but in the private sphere: "It was a matter of decorum, at least, if not of morality, in both Jewish and Greco-Roman society that women exercised power and influence in private rather than in public."[43]

Although Apollos was highly educated, he listened. He could have arrogantly rejected this couple's teaching. Lenski comments on the role reversal:

Who were these humble people to teach a university
graduate, this orator schooled in the Scriptures? ...
He must have been a man of deep spirituality not to
let his superior education, ability, and standing assert
themselves and prevent him from going to school to
such lowly teachers. He is an example for all the high
and mighty men of education today and for the green
beginners for whom a little learning is already a dangerous thing. They scorn the old faith, look down even
upon godly parents who cling to it and on the church
that keeps the sacred fire burning. Apollos shall judge
them at that day![44]

After learning the gospel more accurately, Apollos traveled
to Achaia and "greatly helped those who had believed through
grace; for he vigorously refuted the Jews publicly, showing
from the Scriptures that Jesus is the Christ" (Acts 18:27-28). John
MacArthur proposes, "He exploded like a bombshell on Corinth's
unconverted Jewish community. ... [H]e crushed his opponents,
totally disproving them at every point."[45] What powerful fruit
from the work of Priscilla and Aquila! Imagine the losses to the
kingdom if they had refused to reach out.

Scripture reveals little about Priscilla's later life. She and Aquila
moved back to Rome, probably after Claudius died and the edict
banning Jews was lifted (A.D. 55). Paul greeted these "fellow
workers in Christ Jesus, who risked their own necks for my life"
and "the church that is in their house" in his Roman letter (A.D. 57;
Romans 16:3-5). J. Barmby suggests that the "risk" may mean
Priscilla and Aquila "shielded Paul from the wrath and violence
of enemies of the faith" during the Jewish insurrection in Achaia
(Acts 18:12ff) or in Ephesus when Demetrius the silversmith
raised a tumult (19:23ff).[46]

The couple eventually moved back to Ephesus. Paul saluted
them in his second letter to Timothy (A.D. 66-67). *The New Open
Bible* notes, "Priscilla and Aquila (2 Timothy 4:19) probably returned from Rome (Romans 16:3) to Ephesus after the burning

of Rome and the beginning of the persecution."[47]

Priscilla and Aquila sacrificed for the gospel, showed hospitality, taught Apollos, hosted church assemblies and risked their lives. Doyle Roth writes, "Many in the church do not possess the leadership gifts that Paul and Apollos had, but they might have the quiet servant gifts like Aquila and Priscilla. Paul's ministry would have struggled without the important ministry offered by this couple."[48] These fellow workers lived together, worked together, and – tradition says – died together, beheaded for their faith outside the walls of Rome.[49]

Priscilla is an example for Christian women today. Lockyer suggests that Aquila must have praised God for such a precious gifted wife.[50] My songwriter friend, Jean, presents an ideal modern Christian woman engaged in evangelistic efforts with her husband, humbly and in all propriety. Who knows how many future ministers in their fourth-grade class are – even now – being taught the gospel more accurately.

Reflection Questions

1. Discuss the three biblical evidences of marital devotion between Priscilla and Aquila.

2. List ministry activities in which Priscilla participated.

3. Describe Apollos' background (secular and religious).

4. When Apollos preached in the synagogue, why did Priscilla and Aquila take him aside?

5. What can you do to become more evangelistic?

Spiritual Exercise

Write down the names of people you know who need the gospel. Pray for an opportunity to talk to them about Christ.

Chapter 3

Follow the Holy Women

1 Peter 3:6

The Bible is full of godly examples for Christian women. Sarah is one whose daughters we are if we "do good" (1 Peter 3:6). She rose above her imperfections and developed a faith worthy of mention in Hebrews 11. God wants us to grow (2 Peter 3:18; Romans 12:2). The 12 women in this study demonstrate that maturity-building exercises like prayer, Bible study and service can help us transform into Christ's image (8:29; 2 Corinthians 3:18).

This concluding chapter is a review of previous lessons. It compares and contrasts the lives of the 12 women and their exercises to discover what may apply in our personal journeys toward maturity. My prayer is that you will be inspired to engage in the same tools.

In our examination of these women, we find three overarching elements aiding their maturity. First, each faced an "interruption" in her daily routine of life – a "trial." Some events were good; others were difficult to endure. Second, each woman made a decision to seek God's help and blessings by participating in specific disciplines. Finally, we see that God played a role in each trial, discipline and transformation. For example, Mary of

Bethany was interrupted by Jesus' visit. She welcomed the opportunity to listen to Him, and she grew in love and faith. Rahab received the two spies. She acknowledged Jehovah as God and chose to hide the men. Not only were she and her family saved, but God allowed her to become part of Israel's family.

This three-element concept comes from Dallas Willard's "Golden Triangle" curriculum of Christlikeness (1998). The following illustration is based on his theory of spiritual growth:[1]

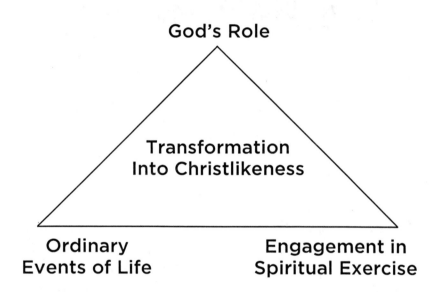

God's Role

Transformation Into Christlikeness

Ordinary Events of Life

Engagement in Spiritual Exercise

Willard emphasizes God's part in the transformation process:

> The intervention of the Holy Spirit is placed at the apex of the triangle to indicate its primacy in the entire process. The trials of daily life and our activities specially planned for transformation are placed at the bottom to indicate that where the transformation is actually carried out is in our real life, where we dwell with God and our neighbors. And at the level of real life, the role of what is imposed upon us ("trials") goes hand in hand with our choices as to what we will do with ourselves.[2]

Let's examine these elements through the lives of our 12 subjects and view our personal transformation possibilities in light of theirs.

Ordinary Events of Life

John MacArthur describes some biblical models as "ordinary, common, and in some cases shockingly low-caste women."[3] This applies to most of the women in our study. Rahab was a heathen prostitute, and Hagar was a pagan slave. Aren't we glad God sees our open hearts (1 Samuel 16:7)? He also accepts geographical and societal transplants. Sarah followed Abraham to a foreign land, Jochebed and Miriam were Hebrew captives in Egypt, and Esther was a Jewish orphan in Persia. How many of us have been uprooted, learning that this world is not our home? Not many of our subjects lived in spiritually encouraging surroundings. Hannah and Naomi lived during the evil days of the judges, and Mary of Nazareth bore social rejection in her virgin pregnancy. Scripture provides little background for Mary of Bethany, Dorcas and Priscilla. We know only that they followed Jesus' teachings.

We can relate to these 12 women. Like us, they struggled with ordinary events of life, such as physical issues, relationships and losses. Willard calls these "trials." Such challenges can be opportunities for spiritual growth. Our subjects accepted their challenges by participating in maturity-building exercises: prayer, Bible study, service, etc.

Six of the women received opportunities to serve. Jesus needed rest and refreshment from Mary of Bethany. The Israelite spies sought refuge in Rahab's house. Mary of Nazareth was commissioned to bear a special son. Esther was asked to intervene on behalf of her people. Miriam filled the role of women's leader after God delivered Israel from Egypt. Priscilla and her husband taught Apollos, who was preaching an incomplete gospel. Each of these events was an unexpected interruption in life.

Do we welcome opportunities to serve? Hebrews 13:2 urges, "Do not forget to entertain strangers, for by so doing some have unwittingly entertained angels." Who knows what blessings God has planned for us as we assist in His work? The disciplines of Bible study, hospitality, submission, fasting, worship in song and evangelism are growth-producing activities.

This study also has illustrated that difficult situations (trials) can help us grow. James urged, "My brethren, count it all joy when you fall into various trials" because such testing builds spiritual maturity (James 1:2-4). The other six of our subjects incurred tragic circumstances. Some immediately placed their trust in God, while others dragged their feet as God worked in their lives.

Like most married women, Hannah and Sarah expected to have children. Scripture tells us that God had closed Hannah's womb. He had a delayed plan for Sarah. But Sarah followed the custom of her day and used her handmaid as a surrogate. This prompted Hagar's two flights: (1) to escape abuse in Genesis 16 and (2) to obey Sarah's demand to leave in Genesis 21. Both resulted in wilderness solitude. During her second experience, in solitude, Hagar anticipated the death of her son, Ishmael. Jochebed had a different plan for her son despite Pharaoh's edict to cast him into the Nile.

Death can be the greatest tragedy we face. Naomi suffered the loss of her husband and her sons while in Moab. Acts 9 introduces Dorcas, then quickly states "she became sick and died" (v. 37).

Just as today, women living in Bible times faced infertility, abuse, fear and death. Some of these events had natural causes. In other cases, God removed the protective hedge and allowed trials to occur. Some suggest Naomi's trials were precipitated by sin.[4] We all know women who, through their own actions, cause difficult circumstances like broken relationships, illness and death. It is important to study and apply the God-given means for spiritual growth.

Engagement in Spiritual Exercises

Spiritual maturity is not automatic. It requires personal effort. John Ortberg asserts, "Authentic spiritual transformation begins with training, discipline."[5] The term "Spiritual Disciplines" is used in spiritual formation literature to describe Bible study, prayer, service, and other maturity-building exercises. Some believe that "discipline" has a negative connotation, but we know self-discipline is required for spiritual growth.

We may conclude that although all the women did not initiate the practice of spiritual exercises, each made a deliberate choice to continue in them. Human free agency is an important concept. In the midst of trials, one can refuse to act and accept physical, emotional or spiritual defeat – or one can seek God's will and be blessed.

Most of these women faced their trials with unwavering trust in God. Jochebed, Hannah, Rahab, Mary of Bethany and Mary of Nazareth – immediately and wholeheartedly – grabbed their opportunities to engage in maturity-building disciplines. By faith Jochebed hid her son for three months and then let him go. Hannah kept a godly attitude and poured out her heart in prayer. Rahab hid the spies as the king's soldiers approached her door. Mary of Bethany refused to be distracted because she knew Jesus' words offered spiritual nourishment. When Gabriel explained God's plan to Mary of Nazareth, she submissively responded, "Let it be to me according to your word" (Luke 1:38).

Dorcas and Priscilla also may have quickly accepted opportunities to serve. Dorcas was converted and made clothing for needy widows not long after the church was established. Priscilla heard Apollos in the synagogue and immediately taught him the gospel more accurately.

Hagar is an unusual case. She did not go into the wilderness to find God; she was driven there first by fear and then by force. However, she was overwhelmed by the Lord's compassion, and she obeyed His instructions. It must have been difficult to return to Sarah. Do we find it easy to take aside the lost and uninformed to teach them the gospel?

Immediacy and wholeheartedness describe some of the responses to God's call by these 12 women. When Esther, Sarah and Naomi faced trials, they waited before acting. Esther first considered the consequences of approaching the king. At Mordecai's wake-up call, she initiated a fast. Sarah waited years for a son.

When she gave up hope of conceiving, she sent her husband into Hagar's bed, which produced disastrous results. It took the Lord's strengthening visit for Sarah to receive "strength to conceive seed, and she bore a child when she was past the age, because she judged Him faithful who had promised" (Hebrews 11:11). When Naomi lost her husband and sons, she declared, "[T]he hand of the LORD has gone out against me!" (Ruth 1:13). She became bitter and told the women of Bethlehem, "[T]he Almighty has afflicted me" (v. 21). Through the love of Ruth and Boaz, Naomi overcame her grief and accepted God's blessings again.

Miriam is also an unusual case. Scripture does not reveal when she began to worship God in song, but we may assume she learned faith from her mother, Jochebed. However, her later rebellion against Moses reflects a heart not wholly devoted to God. Miriam is the only woman in our study who first served as a model but then fell into sinful behavior.

Each of our subjects encountered a trial in the midst of ordinary, everyday life. Each had a choice to say, "No, I will not accept this interruption" or to say, "Yes, Lord, Thy will be done." God, who sees open hearts, makes His way inside, provides opportunities for maturity-building exercises, and plays a role in transformation.

God's Role

When Paul commanded transformation in Romans 12:2, he used the passive voice. Instead of saying, "Transform yourselves," he urged us to "be transformed."[6] According to Scripture and literature on spiritual maturity, inner transformation is God's work; but Christians must participate in the process. Donald S. Whitney asserts that "the God-given means" to promote spiritual growth is to engage in spiritual disciplines.[7] Richard Foster concurs:

> The Disciplines are God's way of getting us into the ground: they put us where he can work within us and transform us. … The inner righteousness we seek is not something that is poured on our heads. God has

ordained the Disciplines of the spiritual life as the means by which we place ourselves where he can bless us.[8]

Willard emphasizes the Holy Spirit in his "curriculum for Christlikeness." However, all three members of the Godhead – God the Father, God the Son and the Holy Spirit – may be found in our subjects' transformation.[9]

God was involved personally in the accounts of Sarah, Hagar, Mary of Nazareth and Mary of Bethany. He directly promised Abraham a son (Genesis 12:1ff) and later reaffirmed Sarah's part with her sacramental name (17:15-16). When she remained in doubt, He strengthened her faith through a visit (18:10). Then He opened her womb. "And the LORD visited Sarah as He had said, and the LORD did for Sarah as He had spoken. For Sarah conceived and bore Abraham a son in his old age" (21:1-2). Sarah's body was unable to reproduce on its own. Donald Guthrie notes, "In view of her advancing years she needed some power (dynamis) beyond herself if she was to conceive and bring forth a child."[10]

During Hagar's first solitude, "the Angel of the LORD" approached her (Genesis 16:7). Whitelaw suggests that "the angel of Jehovah" was "the incarnation of the God-Man."[11] He knew about her ill treatment and promised to help her. He covenanted with her to bless the son in her womb. During Hagar's second solitude, He reaffirmed His covenant blessing (21:17-18). He opened Hagar's eyes so she could see a nearby well. God's Word directs us to life solutions and spiritual nourishment today if we will but open our eyes and read His Word.

Jesus the Son came to Bethany and offered words of life to Martha and Mary. Mary accepted His invitation. She "sat at Jesus' feet and heard His word" (Luke 10:39). He commended her for refusing to be distracted and for choosing "the good part" (v. 42). Mary of Bethany was blessed. We have the same privilege to sit at Jesus' feet through study of the Word.

All three members of the Godhead were involved in the commission of Mary of Nazareth to bear the Messiah. Jehovah found favor in her and promised to be with her (Luke 1:28-30). Mary submitted to His will. The Holy Ghost overshadowed her, and she conceived "the Son of the Highest" (v. 32). Raymond Brown beautifully explains, "Mary's conception involves a divine creative action without human intercourse; it is the work of the overshadowing Spirit, that same Spirit that hovered at the creation of the world when all was void (Genesis 1:2)."[12] Then, "when the fullness of the time had come, God sent forth His Son" (Galatians 4:4), and Mary bore the Christ child. What special and unique opportunities have come your way?

Of course, it was Gabriel whom God sent to Mary. God often used messengers to offer opportunities of service. Both Rahab and Esther were approached by representatives of God's people. William H. Willimon suggests, "Rahab was minding her own business, looking after things in her place when the Lord, through two frightened spies, asked her to mind his business for a change."[13] She acted out of fear and respect for Jehovah. Merling asserted that "in her words, she claims YHWH as her God."[14] As a result, Rahab was "justified" (James 2:25). After the destruction of Jericho, God accepted her into Israel and placed her in the lineage of Christ (Matthew 1:5).

Deity does not always work in ways that are visible. His "hiddenness" is just as effective as His direct approaches. Dave Bland points out in the book of Esther:

> His hiddenness develops the faith and trust of his people. The writer does not know of a particular realm of creation and history that is outside divine direction. Instead, it is implied that God uses even the smallest "accidental" detail for his purposes. At the same time there is no implication that this total control in any way limits the freedom of activity of the characters involved. "The guiding hand is not seen as the moving finger."[15]

God's name appears nowhere in the account, but His providence is evident. Esther's favor with the king of Persia may imply "God had quietly paved the way" for her reception.[16]

Some propose that Mordecai alluded to God in his statement that relief and deliverance would arise for the Jews "from another place" (Esther 4:14). Jon D. Levenson suggests that the Greek manuscript tradition of the *Alpha Text of Esther* "apparently had explicit religious language ... God will be their help and deliverance."[17] Bland adds that the Hebrew *maqom* may be a substitute for the divine name.[18] Perhaps the writer wanted readers to consider God's care. After Israel's fast for Esther, might God have moved the king's heart? (Proverbs 21:1).

Hiddenness also may describe God's help for Naomi. Ruth 2:3 states that Ruth "happened to come to the part of the field belonging to Boaz." However, countered Bland, "[I]t hardly seems likely that in the midst of God's activity in the characters' lives there should be a place for 'luck.'"[19] Naomi blamed her calamities on God. Yet when Boaz allowed Ruth to glean his field, Naomi attributed it to God's kindness. When Obed was born, the women of Bethlehem praised God for providing restoration to Naomi's life.

Jehovah, whom Eli the priest called "the God of Israel," heard Hannah's prayer and opened her womb (1 Samuel 1:17). Walter Brueggemann observed, "Yahweh is the key factor in the narrative. The son is born only because Yahweh remembered. Everything depends on asking Yahweh and being answered by Yahweh."[20] Hannah acknowledged this by naming her son Samuel, which means "heard of God."

We may assume that Jochebed approached God in prayer on behalf of her son. Hebrews 11:23 says that "by faith" Moses' parents hid him. God's providence can be seen throughout Moses' life as he was "learned in all the wisdom of the Egyptians" and sent by God "to be a ruler and a deliverer" (Acts 7:22, 35). Miriam also approached God as she led the women with these words: "Sing to the LORD, For He has triumphed gloriously!" (Exodus 15:21). God had chosen Miriam to be prophetess and leader among the women of Israel: "For I brought you up from the land of Egypt, I redeemed you from the house of bondage; And I sent before you Moses, Aaron, and Miriam" (Micah 6:4;

Exodus 15:20). When she rebelled against Moses, Jehovah Himself called her out and punished her. God dealt directly and swiftly with people under the old Mosaic covenant.

Under the Christian covenant He speaks through the Holy Scriptures (2 Timothy 3:15-17). God dwells with us (2 Corinthians 6:16), Jesus promised to be with us (Matthew 28:20), and the Holy Spirit "makes intercession for us" (Romans 8:26). Dorcas and Priscilla lived in the Christian dispensation. God worked through Dorcas' talents as a seamstress. However, He chose to resurrect her in order that her Christian influence would increase. After Peter raised her, "it became known throughout all Joppa, and many believed on the Lord" (Acts 9:42). Priscilla also spent her Christian life in God's service by opening her home for worship and in working with her husband and Paul. Scripture emphasizes Priscilla's evangelism in teaching Apollos. Jesus promised also to be with us in our evangelistic efforts (Matthew 28:20).

Transformation Toward Spiritual Maturity

Willard proposes that if Christians engage in spiritual disciplines during trials, God will create within them a renewed heart centered in the mind of Christ. Such transformation should be our goal (Romans 12:2; 8:29). The biblical accounts in our study show a correlation between maturity-building exercises and spiritual transformation. With God's help, each shows some degree of spiritual growth in Christlike actions and attitudes – except one. Miriam eventually allowed egotism to choke out her faith and service.

Some of these women may be expected to show more growth than others. Hagar, Ruth and Rahab were pagans who at first did not know the Lord. Sarah's knowledge of God may have come "secondhand" through Abraham until the Lord's visit. Naomi and Esther were born into God's family but showed little faith in Him – until He worked in their lives. Hannah, Mary of Bethany and Mary of Nazareth were godly women who increased in maturity through a closer relationship with Deity. The biblical accounts of Jochebed, Dorcas and Priscilla present only a snapshot of their faith; yet their specific acts of obedience promoted a godly influence,

These women could not have grown spiritually by their effort alone. MacArthur agrees:

> [A]ll these women ultimately became extraordinary not because of any natural qualities of their own, but because the one true God whom they worshiped is great, mighty, glorious, and awesome, and He refined them like silver. He redeemed them through the work of an extraordinary Savior – His own divine Son – and conformed them to His image (Romans 8:29). In other words, the gracious work of God in their lives made each one of these women truly extraordinary.[21]

The practice of spiritual disciplines still produces maturity today. But we must have an open, upright heart and faith in God. Robert Mulholland suggests, "But without God's transforming grace, our disciplines are empty, hollow motions, the form of godliness without the power."[22] According to Willard's Golden Triangle theory, believers who deal with ordinary events (trials) in life by engaging in deliberate exercises can, with God's help, experience transformation toward a spiritually renewed heart.

MacArthur concludes his book with a thought that mirrors the goal and purpose of this study. Concerning the 12 models transformed through the practice of spiritual disciplines, he wrote: "My prayer for you is that as you read this book you will share their faith, imitate their faithfulness, and learn to love the Savior whose work in their lives made them truly extraordinary. Your life can be extraordinary, too, by His wonderful grace."[23] Amen.

Endnotes

Introduction
1 John Ortberg, "True (and False) Transformation," *Leadership* 23 (2002): 104.

2 Robert Plummer, "Are the Spiritual Disciplines of 'Silence and Solitude' Really Biblical?" *Southern Baptist Journal of Theology* 10 (Win. 2006): 4.

Chapter 1
1 Gordon T. Smith, *The Voice of Jesus: Discernment, Prayer, and the Witness of the Spirit* (Downer's Grove: InterVarsity, 2003) 11.

2 John Ellis, "Prayer: Bridging the Gap Between Spirituality and Faith," *The Bridge* 42 (Memphis: Harding U Graduate School of Religion, May 2001): 1.

3 Ellis 1.

4 Bobby Ross Jr., "Study to Examine Why Some Leave the Churches of Christ," *Christian Chronicle* 66 (Mar. 2009): 12.

5 Paul Landon Metler, "Exploring a Relationship Between Spiritual Practice and Christian Character Development," diss., Regent University, 2003, 99-100. Shaena Engle, "College Students' Spirituality and Religiousness Vary by Race and Gender," 6 Oct. 2005, U of

California, 21 Jan. 2010 <http://www.universityofcalifornia.edu/news/article/7540>.

6 Charlton Hillis, "Women's Bible Classes: Fluff or Substance?" *Gospel Advocate* (Mar. 2002): 21.

7 Hillis 21.

8 Kevin Leman, *The New Birth Order Book: Why You Are the Way You Are* (Grand Rapids: Revell, 1998) 15.

9 R.C.H. Lenski, *The Interpretation of St. Luke's Gospel* (Minneapolis: Augsburg, 1961, 1943) 612-13.

10 Lenski, *Luke's Gospel* 612.

11 Eugene H. Peterson, *Christ Plays in a Thousand Places* (Grand Rapids: Eerdmans, 2005) 213.

12 Alfred Plummer, *A Critical and Exegetical Commentary on the Gospel According to St. Luke*, 3rd ed. (New York: Scribner's, 1900) 291.

13 Garret Keizer, "Poor Martha," *Christian Century* 118 (July 2001): 14.

14 Lenski, *Luke's Gospel* 617.

15 Adele Ahlberg Calhoun, *Spiritual Disciplines Handbook: Practices That Transform Us* (Downers Grove: InterVarsity, 2005) 165.

16 Anthony J. Fischetto, *Transformed: Intimacy With God* (Shillington: Alpha Omega Counseling Center Inc., 2000) 52.

17 Fischetto 51.

18 Rosemary W. McKnight, *I Love Me, I Love Me Not* (Montgomery: self-published, 1984) 59-61.

19 William F. Arndt and F. Wilbur Gingrich, *A Greek-English Lexicon of the New Testament and Other Early Christian Literature*, 2nd ed. (Chicago: U of Chicago, 1957, 1979) 809.

20 Martel Pace, "Indications of Immaturity: Hebrews 5:11-14," *Truth for Today* 26 (Jan. 2006): 23.

21 J. Ramsey Michaels, "John 12:1-11," *Interpretation* 43 (July 1989): 288.

22 Herbert Lockyer, *All the Women of the Bible* (Grand Rapids: Zondervan, 1967) 105.

23 Lenski, *Luke's Gospel* 619.

24 Fischetto 172.

Chapter 2

1   Charles W. Carter, *Hebrews: The Wesleyan Bible Commentary*, vol. 6 (Grand Rapids: Eerdmans, 1966) 147.

2   Kenneth D. Mulzac, "Hannah: The Receiver and Giver of a Great Gift," *Andrews University Seminary Studies* 40 (2002): 211.

3   Ronald S. Wallace, *Hannah's Prayer and Its Answer* (Grand Rapids: Eerdmans, 2002) 10.

4   Stanley Sayers, "Reflecting on Preaching and Praying," *The Preacher's Periodical* (May 1986): 3.

5   Mulzac 215.

6   Alfred Lord Tennyson, "Morte D'Arthur," *Selections From Tennyson*, ed. William Clyde DeVane and Mabel Phillips DeVane (New York: Crofts, 1947) 57.

7   Carol Meyers, *Women in Scripture: A Dictionary of Named and Unnamed Women in the Hebrew Bible* (Grand Rapids: Eerdmans, 2001) 90.

8   Bill T. Arnold, *The NIV Application Commentary: 1 and 2 Samuel* (Grand Rapids: Zondervan, 2003) 56.

9   R. Payne Smith, *The Pulpit Commentary*, ed. H.D.M. Spence and Joseph S. Exell, vol. 4, 1 Samuel (Grand Rapids: Eerdmans, 1962) 12.

10 Walter Brueggemann, *Interpretation: A Bible Commentary for Teaching and Preaching – First and Second Samuel*, ed. James L. Mays (Louisville: John Knox, 1990) 13.

11 Hans Wilhelm Hertzberg, *1 and 2 Samuel: A Commentary* (Philadelphia: Westminster, 1964) 25.

12 Andrew W. Blackwood, *Leading in Public Prayer* (New York: Abingdon, 1958) 27.

13 R. McKnight, *I Love Me* 60-61.

14 Richard J. Foster, *Celebration of Discipline: The Path to Spiritual Growth*, 3rd ed. (San Francisco: HarperCollins, 1998) 33.

15 Wallace 6.

16 Foster 33.

17 Wallace 12.

18 Wallace 8.

19 http://www.pinkpoem.com/inspirationalpoems/songsofhope/childofmine-dth.html

20 Mulzac 207.

Chapter 3

1 Foster 49.

2 John M. Wiebe, "Esther 4:14: Will Relief and Deliverance Arise for the Jews From Another Place?" *The Catholic Biblical Quarterly* 53 (July 1991): 412. Wiebe states that "the Hebrew *leqahah lo lebat*, 'to take oneself for a daughter,' is strikingly similar to a standard adoption formula employed in Mesopotamia, *ana maruti lequ*, 'to take into the status of sonship.'"

3 F. LaGard Smith, *The Narrated Bible in Chronological Order* (Eugene: Harvest House, 1984) 1234. The 70 years prophesied may be from the fall of Jerusalem (586 B.C.) until the temple was rebuilt (516 B.C.). The captivity lasted 70 years from the first deportation in 605 B.C.

4 Forrest S. Weiland, "Literary Clues to God's Providence in the Book of Esther" *Bibliotheca sacra* 160 (Jan.-Mar. 2003): 37.

5 Smith 1276. George L. Murphy, "Providence and Passion in Esther," *Currents in Theology and Mission* 29 (Apr. 2002): 123.

6 Michael V. Fox, *Character and Ideology in the Book of Esther*, 2nd ed. (Grand Rapids: Eerdmans, 1991) 197.

7 Weiland 39.

8 Fox 198.

9 Lewis Bayles Paton, *A Critical and Exegetical Commentary on the Book of Esther* (1908; Edinburgh: T&T Clark, 1976) 220. This law was designed to give him dignity and to protect him from assassination.

10 Dave Bland, "God's Activity as Reflected in the Books of Ruth and Esther" *Restoration Quarterly* 24 (1981): 141.

11 Weiland 37.

12 Iain Duguid, "But Did They Live Happily Ever After? The Eschatology of the Book of Esther," *Westminster Theological Journal* 68 (2006): 89.

13 Leland Ryken, *How to Read the Bible as Literature and Get More Out of It* (Grand Rapids: Zondervan, 1984) 39.

14 Fox 197.

15 Karen H. Jobes, *The NIV Application Commentary: Esther* (Grand Rapids: Zondervan, 1999) 137.

16 Calhoun 220.

17 Bland 141.

18 William E. Burrows, *The Preacher's Complete Homiletic Commentary on the Book of Esther* (Grand Rapids: Baker, 1978) 156.

19 Walter Elwell, ed., *Evangelical Dictionary of Theology*, 1984 ed., s.v. "Fast, Fasting," by R.D. Linder.

20 Carole Garibaldi Rogers, "Fasting Frees Us From Attachment," *National Catholic Reporter* Feb. 2005: 14.

21 John Scott Lambert, "The Easy Yoke of the Disciplined Life," thesis, Heritage Christian University, 2004, 42.

22 Foster 56-61.

23 Foster 57

24 "Fasting," an information sheet compiled by Sue Glenn (Shaklee dealer in Booneville, Miss.) 2. Sue Glenn, personal e-mail 24 Aug. 2009

25 Calhoun 219.

26 Leland Ryken, *Words of Delight: A Literary Introduction to the Bible*, 2nd ed. (Grand Rapids: Baker, 1992) 119.

27 Weiland 46-47.

28 Lottie Beth Hobbs, *Daughters of Eve* (Fort Worth: Harvest, 1963) 157.

29 Duguid 93-94.

30 Foster 50.

31 Fischetto 167.

Chapter 4

1 Joel B. Green, "The Social Status of Mary in Luke 1:5–2:52: A Plea for Methodological Integration," *Biblica* 73 (1992): 464.

2 Darrell L. Bock, *The NIV Application Commentary: Luke* (Grand Rapids: Zondervan, 1996) 59.

3 Raymond E. Brown, "The Annunication to Mary, the Visitation, and the Magnificat (Luke 1:26-56)," *Worship* 62 (May 1988): 252-53.

4 Brown 252-53.

5 Alfred Plummer, *A Critical and Exegetical Commentary on the Gospel of St. Luke* (Edinburgh: T&T Clark, 1900) 21, 26.

6 Bock 68.

7 Foster 132.

8 Qtd. in Lockyer 94.

9 H.D.M. Spence, *The Pulpit Commentary*, ed. H.D.M. Spence and Joseph S. Exell, vol. 16, Luke (Grand Rapids: Eerdmans, 1975) 8.

10 Bock 25.

11 Calhoun 119.

12 Warren W. Wiersbe, *Be Faithful* (Wheaton: Victor, 1981) 33-34.

13 Bock 67.

14 Calhoun 119.

15 John L. Kachelman, "Rationale for Women's Subjection," *Christian Bible Teacher* 37 (Jan. 1993): 20.

16 Spence 8-9.

17 Calhoun 119.

18 Lockyer 94.

19 Lockyer 92-93. At the time of Lockyer's publication in 1967, the name "Mary" had at least 70 different interpretations, and 3.7 million women were named Mary.

20 Spence 9.

21 Lockyer 95.

22 Bock 65.

23 Lockyer 95.

24 Wiersbe 172.

25 Lockyer 93.

Chapter 5

1 Jon M. Walton, "What About Dorcas?" *Christian Century* 124 (17 Apr. 2007): 16.

2 R.C.H. Lenski, *The Interpretation of the Acts of the Apostles* (1934; Minneapolis: Augsburg, 1961) 384.

3 Lenski, *Acts* 384.

4 Hobbs 157.

5 Walton 16.

6 Lockyer 46.

7 Lenski, *Acts* 385.

8 A.C. Hervey, *The Pulpit Commentary*, ed. H.D.M. Spence and Joseph S. Exell, vol. 18, Acts (Grand Rapids: Eerdmans, 1975) 288.

9 Lenski, *Acts* 385.

10 Simon J. Kistemaker, *Exposition of the Acts of the Apostles* (Grand Rapids: Baker, 1990) 361.

11 Lenski, *Acts* 388. He describes the outer garment: "The himation was really a large, oblong piece of cloth, one corner of which was draped over the left shoulder and fastened under the right shoulder. This garment was ample enough to reach to the ground. It generally served as a covering for the sleeper at night."

12 Lenski, *Acts* 387.

13 Lockyer 47.

14 W.M. Statham, *The Pulpit Commentary*, ed. H.D.M. Spence and Joseph S. Exell, vol. 21, 1 Timothy (Grand Rapids: Eerdmans, 1962) 110.

15 Walton 16.

16 Lenski, *Acts* 384.

17 Kistemaker 360.

18 Lenski, *Acts* 385.

19 Lockyer 47.

20 Kistemaker 362.

21 Lenski, *Acts* 386-87.

22 Calhoun 145.

23 Walton 16.

24 Martin Luther King Jr., "MLK on Service (The Drum Major Instinct – Excerpt From His Famous Speech)," *YouTube*, 27 Jan. 2010 <http://www.youtube.com/watch?v= Th733HfJwdo>.

25 Lockyer 46.

26 Larch S. Garrad, "Dorcas Society," *A Manx Note Book*, 27 Jan. 2010 <http://www.isle-of-man.com/manxnotebook/history/poor/dorcas.htm>.

27 Lockyer 48.

28 June Wesley, "A Lonely Widow" *20th Century Christian* 51 (1 Apr. 1989): 18.

Chapter 6
1 David Merling, "Rahab: The Woman Who Fulfilled the Word of YHWH," *Andrews University Seminary Studies* 41 (Spr. 2003): 34.

2 Elie Assis, "The Choice to Serve God and Assist His People: Rahab and Yael," *Biblica* 85 (2004): 83.

3 Gary A. Rendsburg, "Unlikely Heroes: Women as Israel," *Bible Review* 19 (Feb. 2003): 20.

4 Assis 83.

5 Merling 36.

6 Jane Schaberg, "Before Mary: The Ancestresses of Jesus," *Bible Review* 20 (Dec. 2004): 16.

7 Bryant Wood, "The Walls of Jericho," *Answers in Genesis* (Mar. 1999). 5 Mar. 2010 <http://www.answersingenesis.org/home/area/magazines/docs/v21n2_jericho.asp>.

8 Wood.

9 Footnote for 1 Kings 16:34, *The New Open Bible, NKJV Study Edition* (Nashville: Nelson, 1990).

10 Ajith Fernando, *The NIV Application Commentary: Acts* (Grand Rapids: Zondervan, 1998) 314-15.

11 Eugene H. Peterson, *Christ Plays in Ten Thousand Places* (Grand Rapids: Eerdmans, 2005) 214-15.

12 Laurel Sewell, *The Six Gifts of Hospitality* (Nashville, Gospel Advocate, 2003) 35.

13 Sewell 34.

14 Sewell 33.

15 Benjamin Franklin, "*Poor Richard's Almanack*: More Than 600 Proverbs From 1734 to 1747," *Independence Hall*, ed. Rich Hall, Independence Hall Organization, 17 Jan. 2011 <http://richhall.com/poor_richard. htm>.

16 Sewell 19.

17 Liz Curtis Higgs, "Rahab: A Hooker With a Heart for God," *Today's Christian Woman* 30 (Jan.-Feb. 2008): 55.

18 John MacArthur, *Twelve Extraordinary Women: How God Shaped Women of the Bible and What He Wants to Do With You* (Nashville: Nelson, 2005) 66.

19 Allen Verhey, "Is Lying Always Wrong?" *Christianity Today* 43 (24 May 1999): 68.

20 C.F. Keil and Franz Delitzsch, *Commentary on the Old Testament*, vol. 2 (1866; Peabody: Hendrickson, 1996) 27.

21 K.M. Campbell, "Rahab's Covenant: A Short Note on Joshua ii. 9-21," *Vetus testamentum* 22 (Apr. 1972): 244.

22 Merling 31.

23 Raymond E. Brown, "Rachab in Matt.1:5 Probably Is Rahab of Jericho" *Biblica* 63 (1982): 79.

24 William H. Willimon, "Best Little Harlot's House in Jericho," *Christian Century* 100 (Oct. 1983): 957.

Chapter 7

1 Lockyer 156.

2 Hobbs 19.

3 Donald Guthrie, *The Letter to the Hebrews: An Introduction and Commentary* (Grand Rapids: Eerdmans, 1983) 232.

4 Lockyer 158.

5 Eugenia Price, *God Speaks to Women Today* (Grand Rapids: Zondervan, 1964) 26.

6 Charme Robarts, "Contours of Faith: Abraham and Sarah as Our Partners in Disciple-Making" *Leaven* 11 (Jul. 2003): 132.

7 John H. Walton, *The NIV Application Commentary: Genesis* (Grand Rapids: Zondervan, 2001) 500.

8 John T. Willis, *Genesis* (Austin: Sweet, 1979) 239.

9 Walton 446.

10 Walton 454.

11 Walton 454.

12 Willis 241-42.

13 Katherine L. Cook, "Laughter of Hope, Laughter of Joy: A Mother's Day Sermon" *Christian Ministry* 17 (May 1986): 31.

14 Thomas Whitelaw, *The Pulpit Commentary*, ed. H.D.M. Spence and Joseph S. Exell, vol. 1, Genesis-Exodus (Grand Rapids: Eerdmans, 1962) 226.

15 Lockyer 62.

16 George Van Pelt Campbell, "Rushing Ahead of God: An Exposition of Genesis 16:1-16," *Bibliotheca sacra* 163 (July-Sep. 2006): 285.

17 Guy N. Woods, *Biblical Backgrounds of the Troubled Middle East* (Nashville: Gospel Advocate, 1991) 20.

18 Richard A. Spencer, "Hebrews 11:1-3, 8-16," *Interpretation* 49 (July 1995): 239.

19 Neale Pryor, "Abraham: Believing the Promises," *Harding University Lectures*, vol. 68 (Searcy: Harding U, 1991) 55.

20 Rosemary W. McKnight, *Those Who Wait* (Nashville: Gospel Advocate, 1989) 2.

21 R. McKnight, *Those Who Wait* 3.

22 Irene C. Taylor, "Sarah – Sarai," *East Tennessee School of Preaching Lectures* (Knoxville: ETSP, 1996): 132.

23 Lockyer 158.

24 Whitelaw 236.

25 Lockyer 155.

26 C.F. Keil and Franz Delitzsch, *The Pentateuch: Commentary on the Old Testament in Ten Volumes*, trans. James Martin, vol. 1 (Grand Rapids: Eerdmans, 1956) 228.

27 Bruce K. Waltke, *Genesis: A Commentary* (Grand Rapids: Zondervan, 2001) 268.

28 Don Seeman, " 'Where Is Sarah Your Wife?': Cultural Poetics of Gender and Nationhood in the Hebrew Bible," *Harvard Theological Review* 91 (Apr. 1998): 112.

29 Bobbie C. Jobe, *Sarah's Story* (Abilene: Quality, 1986) 38.

30 Charles L. Brown, "Sarah, an Example for Modern Women," *East Tennessee School of Preaching Lectures* 27 (Knoxville: ETSP, 2001): 476.

31 Spencer 242.

32 Waltke 268.

33 John H. Tietjen, "Hebrews 11:8-12," *Interpretation* 42 (Oct. 1988): 404.

34 Nick Hamilton, "Sarah Waited on God – Hebrews 11:11," *Freed-Hardeman Lectures*, ed. David Lipe (Henderson: Freed-Hardeman U, 2001): 160.

Chapter 8
1 Campbell 285.

2 Keil and Delitzsch, *The Pentateuch*, vol. 1, 219.

3 Whitelaw 225.

4   Katherine L. Cook, "Laughter of Hope, Laughter of Joy: A Mother's Day Sermon," *Christian Ministry* 17 (May 1986): 31.

5   Lockyer 61.

6   Whitelaw 226.

7   Whitelaw 226.

8   Lockyer 62.

9   James C. Okoye, "Sarah and Hagar: Genesis 16 and 21," *Journal for the Study of the Old Testament* 32 (2007): 167.

10 Whitelaw 226.

11 Whitelaw 228. He presents a long list of scholars who concur.

12 Jan Johnson, *Spiritual Disciplines Companion: Bible Studies and Practices to Transform Your Soul* (Downers Grove: InterVarsity, 2009) 15.

13 Foster 96.

14 Johnson 19.

15 Corinne S. Elkins, "Sarah, Woman of Faith," *Memphis School of Preaching Lectures*, ed. Dub McClish (Memphis: MSP, 2001): 961.

16 Okoye 169.

17 Okoye 171.

18 R. Plummer 4.

19 Thomas H. Leale, *The Preacher's Complete Homiletic Commentary on the First Book of Moses Called Genesis: Chapters 9-50*, ed. Joseph S. Exell and Thomas H. Leale (Grand Rapids: Baker, 1978) 454.

20 Calhoun 113.

21 Peterson 156.

22 Foster 102.

23 Foster 102.

24 R. Plummer 9.

25 Foster 21.

26 Leale 454.

27 Leale 454-55.

28 Calhoun 113.

29 Leale 455.

30 Leale 456.

31 James Montgomery Boice, *Genesis: An Expositional Commentary*, vol. 2 (Grand Rapids: Baker, 1998) 573.

Chapter 9

1 Brian Weinstein, "Naomi's Mission: A Commentary on the Book of Ruth," *Jewish Bible Quarterly* 32 (Jan.-Mar. 2004): 46.

2 Charles P. Baylis, "Naomi in the Book of Ruth in Light of the Mosaic Covenant," *Bibliotheca sacra* 161 (Oct.-Dec. 2004): 420.

3 Baylis 415, footnote 11.

4 Peter W. Coxon, "Was Naomi a Scold?" *Journal for the Study of the Old Testament* 14 (Oct. 1989): 29.

5 Baylis 424.

6 James Morison, *The Pulpit Commentary*, ed. H.D.M. Spence and Joseph S. Exell, vol. 4, Ruth (Grand Rapids: Eerdmans, 195) 20.

7 Ronald T. Hyman, "Questions and Changing Identity in the Book of Ruth," *Union Seminary Quarterly Review* 39 (1984): 193.

8 Granger E. Westberg, *Good Grief* (Philadelphia: Fortress, 1971) 11-44.

9 Vickie Ramsey Greenway, *Humor 'n' Healing* (Pulaski: Sain, 2004) 78.

10 Raymond E. Brown, "Rachab in Matt. 1:5 Probably Is Rahab of Jericho," *Biblica* 63 (1982): 79.

11 Keil and Delitzsch, *Old Testament*, vol. 2, 352.

12 Hobbs 95.

13 Keil and Delitzsch, *Old Testament*, vol. 2, 353.

14 Morison 46.

15 Morison 47. Morison defines "winnowing" as "throwing up the grain with a fork against the wind, by which the chaff and broken straw were dispersed and the grain fell to the ground."

16 Baylis 429.

17 Keil and Delitzsch, *Old Testament*, vol. 2, 353. Baylis adds that instead of referring to Boaz with the legal term for "next of kin" or "redeemer," Naomi used a nonlegal term, "kindred," while Ruth used the legal word at the threshing floor. Baylis cites Brown, Driver and Briggs, *A Hebrew and English Lexicon of the Old Testament*, 145.

18 Morison 69.

19 Weinstein 49. Weinstein states on page 48, "Shaye Cohen tells us that after the conquest of the Promised Land, Jewish, Judahite or Judean identity meant that one lived in Juday-Judea or that one traced one's origins to this geographical entity. One did not have to be a descendant of Judah. In other words, Ruth could become a Judean by moving, marrying, and living there." [Shaye Cohen, *The Beginnings of Jewishness* (Berkeley: U of California, 1999) 87.]

20 Baylis 422.

21 Morison 71.

22 Greenway 120.

23 Greenway 121-22.

Chapter 10

1 Terence E. Fretheim, *Interpretation: A Bible Commentary for Teaching and Preaching – Exodus* (Louisville: John Knox, 1991) 35.

2 George Rawlinson, *The Pulpit Commentary*, ed. H.D.M. Spence and Joseph S. Exell, vol. 1, Exodus (Grand Rapids: Eerdmans, 1962) 17.

3 Rawlinson 17.

4 Fretheim 33-34.

5 C.F. Keil and Franz Delitzsch, *The Pentateuch: Commentary on the Old Testament*, vol. 2, The Second Book of Moses (Peabody: Hendrickson, 1996) 426.

6 John I. Durham, *Exodus: Word Biblical Commentary*, vol. 3 (Waco: Word, 1987) 14.

7 William J. McRae, "The Providence of God," *Emmaus Journal* 3 (1994): 62.

8 Fretheim 32.

9 Joseph S. Exell, *The Preacher's Complete Homiletic Commentary on the Second Book of Moses Called Exodus* (Grand Rapids: Baker, 1996) 17.

10 Durham 16.

11 Rawlinson 24.

12 Cindy Colley, *Women of Deliverance* (Huntsville: Publishing Designs, 2004) 38.

13 Fretheim 37.

14 Tietjen 404.

15 Meyers 90.

16 Coy D. Roper, *Exodus: Truth for Today Commentary* (Searcy: Resource Publications, 2008) 37.

17 Exell 16.

18 McRae 64.

19 Nahum M. Sarna, *Exploring Exodus* (1986; New York: Schocken Books, 1996) 32.

20 R. Alan Cole, *Exodus: An Introduction and Commentary – Tyndale Old Testament Commentaries* (Downers Grove: InterVarsity, 1973) 59.

21 Fretheim 38.

22 Exell 16.

23 Exell 15.

24 Rawlinson 25. McRae 64.

25 McRae 65.

26 Exell 16.

27 Exell 15.

Chapter 11

1 George J. Brooke, "A Long-Lost Song of Miriam," *Biblical Archaeology Review* 20 (May-June 1994): 62.

2 Exell 17.

3 Roper 239.

4 Durham 203.

5 Durham 203.

6 Roper 239.

7 Nahum M. Sarna, *Exodus: The JPS Torah Commentary* (New York: Jewish Publication Society, 1991) 76.

8 Roper 239.

9 Lockyer 112.

10 C.F. Keil and Franz Delitzsch, "Second Book of Moses (Exodus)," *Biblical Commentary on the Old Testament*, trans. James Martin, vol. 2, The Pentateuch (1866; Grand Rapids: Eerdmans,1980) 56.

11 Exell 292.

12 Rawlinson 5. Exell 292.

13 Roper 250.

14 Exell 292.

15 Roper 238.

16 J. Urquhart, *The Pulpit Commentary*, ed. H.D.M. Spence and Joseph S. Exell, vol. 1, Genesis-Exodus, vol. 2, The Book of Exodus (Grand Rapids: Eerdmans, 1962) 18.

17 Fretheim 164.

18 Exell 292.

19 Lockyer 113.

20 Hugo Leichtentritt, *Music, History and Ideas* (Cambridge: Harvard U, 1947) 34.

21 Everett Ferguson, *The Church of Christ: A Biblical Ecclesiology for Today* (Grand Rapids: Eerdmans, 1996) 272.

22 John Chrysostom, *Commentary on the Psalms*, vol. 2, trans. Robert Charles Hill (Brookline: Holy Cross Orthodox, 2007).

23 Curt Sachs, *Our Musical Heritage*, 2nd ed. (Englewood Cliffs: Prentice-Hall, 1955) 43.

24 Rubel Shelly, *Sing His Praise: A Case for A Cappella Music as Worship Today* (Nashville: 20th Century Christian, 1987) 97. Some date the first instrument for Christian worship as an organ given to King Pepin in A.D. 757, or even earlier (102).

25 Joseph Otten, "Musical Instruments in Church Services," *The Catholic Encyclopedia*, vol. 10, 1911, Robert Appleton Co., 23 Jan. 2011 <http://www.newadvent.org/cathen/10657a.htm>. Shelly 91.

26 Shelly 104.

27 Shelly 102, 104.

28 Lockyer 113.

29 C.F. Keil and Franz Delitzsch, "The Fourth Book of Moses (Numbers)," *Commentary on the Old Testament*, vol. 1, The Pentateuch (Grand Rapids: Eerdmans, 1980) 75.

30 Keil and Delitzsch, "Numbers," 77.

31 Phyllis Trible, "Bringing Miriam Out of the Shadows" *Bible Review* (Feb. 1989): 22.

32 Keil and Delitzsch, "Numbers," 75.

33 R. Winterbotham, *The Pulpit Commentary*, ed. H.D.M. Spence and Joseph S. Exell, vol. 2, Numbers (Grand Rapids: Eerdmans, 1962) 132.

34 Keil and Delitzsch, "Numbers," 81.

35 Winterbotham 133.

Chapter 12

1 Lockyer 122.

2 F.F. Bruce, *The Pauline Circle* (Grand Rapids: Eerdmans, 1985) 45.

3 Murray J. Harris, *Slave of Christ: A New Testament Metaphor for Total Devotion to Christ* (Downers Grove: InterVarsity, 1999) 165. Wayne Meeks, *The First Urban Christians* (New Haven: Yale, 1983) 59; qtd. in Moody 97. Lockyer 122. Harris believes she was Gentile. Meeks describes the couple as "Hellenistic Jews." Lockyer suggests that both were Jews, born in Pontus.

4 Harris 161.

5 William O. Walker Jr., "The Portrayal of Aquila and Priscilla in Acts: The Question of Sources," *New Testament Studies* 54 (Oct. 2008): 482.

6 George W. Knight, *The Pastoral Epistles* (Grand Rapids: Eerdmans, 1992) 475-76.

7 Harris 166.

8 Lenski, *Acts* 774-75.

9 Everett Ferguson, *Backgrounds of Early Christianity*, 2nd ed. (Grand Rapids: Eerdmans, 1993) 31-32. C.K. Barrett, *The New Testament Background* (New York: HarperCollins, 1989) 14.

10 Harris 165.

11 Dwight L. Moody, "On the Road Again," *Review and Expositor* 92 (1995): 96.

12 Pliny, *Natural History*, 19:23-24.

13 Harris 165.

14 Lockyer 122.

15 Harris 165.

16 Plutarch ("Advice to Bride and Groom," 19 [140]);" qtd. in Aida Besancon Spencer, "Peter's Pedagogical Method in 1 Peter 3:6," *Bulletin for Biblical Research* 10 (2000): 108.

17 Scot McKnight, *1 Peter: The NIV Application Commentary* (Grand Rapids: Zondervan, 1996) 184.

18 Harris 167.

19 Jerome Murphy-O'Connor, "Prisca and Aquila: Traveling Tentmakers and Church Builders," *Bible Review* 8 (Dec. 1992): 51.

20 Meeks 59; qtd. in *Moody* 97.

21 J. Ernest Runions, "Nobodies of the New Testament: Priscilla & Aquila" *HIS* (Dec. 1978): 19-20.

22 Ajith Fernando, *Acts: The NIV Application Commentary* (Grand Rapids: Zondervan, 1998) 504.

23 Lenski, *Acts* 769. Fernando 504.

24 Lenski, *Acts* 769. He adds, "The rest of his education had been made subservient to the Scriptures and to the power to use them effectively." Joseph A. Fitzmyer, *The Acts of the Apostles: The Anchor Bible* (New York: Doubleday, 1998) 638. John MacArthur, *The MacArthur New Testament Commentary: Acts 13-28* (Chicago: Moody, 1996) 161.

25 Fitzmyer 639. Lenski, *Acts* 771. Lenski adds, "The Jews later called the entire Christian doctrine and practice *derek hanotsarim*, 'the Way of the Christians.' So 'Way' means doctrine, faith, confession, life, all combined."

26 William F. Arndt and F. Wilbur Gingrich, *A Greek-English Lexicon of the New Testament and other Early Christian Literature*, 2nd ed. (Chicago: U of Chicago, 1979) 337.

27 Lenski, *Acts* 772.

28 Lenski, *Acts* 773.

29 Danny Dodds, "New Testament Personalities," *Christian Standard* (Feb. 1997): 23.

30 Dodds 23.

31 Fitzmyer 637.

32 M. Robert Mulholland, *Invitation to a Journey: A Road Map for Spiritual Formation* (Downers Grove: InterVarsity, 1993) 11.

33 George Gallup Jr. and D. Michael Lindsay, *Surveying the Religious Landscape: Trends in U.S. Beliefs* (Harrisburg: Morehouse, 1999): 78.

34 Dan Gilgoff, "Leaving Religion Behind: A Portrait of Nonreligious America," *U.S. News & World Report* 13 Mar. 2009, 4 Mar. 2010

<http://www.usnews.com/articles/news/religion/2009/03/13/leaving-religion-behind-a-portrait-of-nonreligious-america.html>.

35 Gilgoff.

36 Ross 12.

37 Runions 20.

38 Don Humphrey, *Hearts on Fire: A Strategy for Dynamic Evangelism* (Nashville: Gospel Advocate, 1990). Stafford North, *Evangelizing Your Community* (Nashville: 21st Century Christian, 2007).

39 Humphrey 11.

40 North 12.

41 Brad Harrub, *Convicted: A Scientist Examines the Evidence for Christianity* (Brentwood: Focus, 2009).

42 Neil R. Lightfoot, *How We Got the Bible*, 3rd ed. (Grand Rapids: Baker, 2010).

43 Fitzmyer 639. He writes, "The more accurate explanation of the Way would have included its relation to baptism in the Spirit (Christian baptism) and the role it was playing in the implementation of the divine plan of salvation."

44 Moody 97.

45 Lenski, *Acts* 774-75.

46 MacArthur 163.

47 J. Barmby and J. Radford Thomson, *The Pulpit Commentary*, ed. H.D.M. Spence and Joseph S. Exell, vol. 18, Romans (Grand Rapids: Eerdmans, 1950) 455, 459.

48 *The New Open Bible, NKJV Study Edition* (Nashville: Nelson, 1990) 1431.

49 Doyle Roth, "Priscilla and Aquila: Partners in the Gospel" *Christian Standard* (Feb. 2003): 23.

50 Lockyer 124.

51 Lockyer 122.

Chapter 13

1 Dallas Willard, *Divine Conspiracy* (San Francisco: HarperCollins, 1998) 347.

2 Willard 347.

3 MacArthur 9.

4 Baylis 420. He suggests that the Law warned Israelites, like Elimelech, to wholly follow God or they would "perish among the nations, and the land of your enemies shall eat you up" (Leviticus 26:27, 38). Their children likely suffered from the curse of poor health pronounced on the disobedient (Deuteronomy 28:65-66).

5 Ortberg 104.

6 Ortberg 104.

7 Donald S. Whitney, *Spiritual Disciplines for the Christian Life* (Colorado Springs: Navpress, 1991) 17.

8 Foster 7.

9 Willard 347. He explains that the three members of the Trinity are distinguishable in Jesus' baptism scene in Matthew 3:16-17. In the creation account (Genesis 1), the term "Elohim" is plural. God, the Father spoke (v. 3), the Holy Spirit moved (v. 2), and the Son made all things (John 1:1-3).

10 Guthrie 232.

11 Whitelaw 228. He presents a long list of scholars who concur.

12 Brown 252.

13 Willimon 957-58.

14 Merling 43.

15 Bland 136. Weiland 37. Weiland observes, "[T]he tension caused by silence about God's involvement moves the reader to ask, If God was involved, why did He not show up in the story?" He suggests, "If these Jews sought deliverance but not necessarily the Deliverer, then God may have honored their desire by concealing His participation in the events."

16 Weiland 39.

17 Jon D. Levenson, *Esther* (Louisville: Westminster John Knox, 1997) 33. Murphy 124. Murphy describes the Alpha Text as "a Greek manuscript tradition."

18 Bland 140. He also notes, "The majority of scholars are in agreement with this statement."

19 Bland 135-36. He notes, "God is present in every scene, but always in the shadows."

20 Walter Brueggemann, "1 Samuel 1: A Sense of Beginning," *ZAW* 102 (1990): 36; qtd. in Mulzac 216.

21 MacArthur 10.

22 Mulholland 135-36.

23 MacArthur 10.

CPSIA information can be obtained at www.ICGtesting.com
Printed in the USA
LVOW08s1004150713

342869LV00002B/2/P